Backyard Bankers

Praise for this book

'*Backyard Bankers* shows that people themselves have solutions that they own and that work – without a lot of experts trying to tell them or show them what to do. A must read for those who want to help – not harm.'

John Hammock Co-founder of Oxford Poverty and Human Development Initiative (OPHI) and Chair of SOPHIA Oxford United Kingdom

'This book demonstrates clearly the value of money clubs, particularly for newcomers to the United Sates. Benefiting from their experience in various countries in Africa, Latin America, Asia and elsewhere, the authors document the ongoing importance of traditional group finance; how it supports and facilitates economic growth and builds important and useful social capital. And while GDP per capita may be higher in America then many of the countries that come to mind when we think of 'informal finance', this book clearly shows the value and sustainability of these groups and the benefits they bring demonstrating they can and do work anywhere, including America. For anyone interested in understanding the determination, discipline and resourcefulness of immigrants to pursue the American Dream, *Backyard Bankers* is a must read.'

Joanna Ledgerwood, Author of 'The New Microfinance Handbook' and 'Making Market Systems Work for the Poor'

Backyard Bankers

Immigrants, Money Clubs, and the Pursuit of the American Dream

Jeffrey Ashe and Kim Wilson

Practical ACTION PUBLISHING

LAB
LATIN AMERICA BUREAU

Practical Action Publishing Ltd
25 Albert Street, Rugby,
Warwickshire, CV21 2SD, UK
www.practicalactionpublishing.com

A catalogue record for this book is available from the British Library.

A catalogue record for this book has been requested from the Library of Congress.

ISBN 978-1-78853-424-6 Paperback
ISBN 978-1-78853-426-0 Electronic book

Citation: Ashe, J. and Wilson, K. (2024) *Backyard Bankers: Immigrants, Money Clubs, and the Pursuit of the American Dream,* Rugby, UK: Practical Action Publishing http://doi.org/10.3362/9781788534260

Since 1974, Practical Action Publishing has published and disseminated books and information in support of international development work throughout the world.

Practical Action Publishing is a trading name of Practical Action Publishing Ltd (Company Reg. No. 1159018), the wholly owned publishing company of Practical Action. Practical Action Publishing trades only in support of its parent charity objectives and any profits are covenanted back to Practical Action (Charity Reg. No. 247257, Group VAT Registration No. 880 9924 76).

Photo by Jeffrey Ashe.
Photo shows two Guatemalan women in Massachusetts counting funds for their Backyard Bank.

Cover design by Katarzyna Markowska, Practical Action Publishing Typeset by vPrompt eServices, India

The manufacturer's authorised representative in the EU for product safety is Lightning Source France, 1 Av. Johannes Gutenberg, 78310 Maurepas, France. compliance@lightningsource.fr

Contents

Acknowledgements

We want to thank Maria Teresa Nagel, Gene Bianco, Raymond Marolt, Tasfia Zaman, Annie Bright, Charlie Williams, Hannah Campeanu, and Paolo Caglioti – all graduate students at the Fletcher School of Law and Diplomacy at Tufts University. They worked tirelessly to edit these case studies and to search for the literature on money clubs in the United States. We also want to thank our graduate students from Brandeis, Columbia, and Tufts Universities who spent weeks gaining access to immigrant communities to do these interviews, collected the data, and wrote the case studies. These include students from the Sustainable International Development programme at Brandeis University: Pranab Banik who profiled Bangladeshi *shamitis* in Boston, Filimon Ghebretinsae who profiled Eritrean *equobs* in Seattle, Kimlay Lev who profiled Cambodian *tontines* in Lowell and Gail Carter who profiled *sou-sous* in the Barbadian and Haitian communities near Boston. Krishnan Subedi from the Conflict Resolution and Coexistence programme at the Heller School at Brandeis profiled Nepali *dhikutis* in Queens, while Govinda Bahadur Raut, a Hubert H. Humphrey Fellow at Boston University, profiled *dhikutis* in Greater Boston. Elizabeth Mengesha profiled the *iddir* insurance club of Ethiopian cab drivers in Boston. Jayshree Venkatasan profiled a Somalian *ayuuto* in Boston. Bamzi Banchiri profiled a Tanzanian *upato* as well as an insurance club in Boston. Ella Duncan profiled the Burundian ikirimba in Maine. Carolyn M. Musyimi-Kamau profiled Kenyan *chamas* in New Hampshire, and Maria Teresa Nagel profiled *tandas* in Asheville, North Carolina. Aaron Steinberg profiled Haitian *sol* in Boston. Bill Maddocks from the Carsey School of Public Policy at the University of New Hampshire set up and accompanied us on the interviews in Concord, New Hampshire. Dr Dale Adams from Ohio State University and Dr Carlos Vélez-Ibáñez from the School of Transborder Studies, University of Arizona, both experts in the money club field, provided invaluable encouragement and insights as this project progressed.

INTRODUCTION
A few definitions

Whether their traditions hail from Colombia or Cambodia, Bangladesh or Barbados, money clubs in the US adhere to similar structures, principles, and purposes. Before delving into the money club experience, uniquely inhabited by immigrants with American citizens sprinkled into clubs from time to time, we provide a few concepts. Broadly, we encountered three types of clubs, each under the umbrella of a term we call money clubs:

Rotating clubs. These are clubs where, on an appointed date, each member contributes a predetermined amount to the club's coffers. During regular intervals, weekly, bi-weekly, or monthly, depending on the club's rules, one person takes home the contents of the coffers, called a payout or turn.

Insurance clubs. These are clubs where members contribute regular amounts to the club, typically as funeral insurance. The members appoint their beneficiaries and when one passes away the club takes care of the burial costs.

Savings and loan clubs. These are clubs where members pool their money and allow the money to accumulate. They disburse the accumulated funds in the form of loans, usually to members.

Table 1 illustrates these three categories of money clubs, their primary functions, and a few variations. The reader should note that because the money club's membership generates the club's rules, variations are seemingly infinite.

Table 1 Money club type, function, and variations

Club type	Basic functions	Variations
Rotating club (The most common club we studied)	Members contribute money at each interval (weekly, bi-weekly, monthly) based on the club's rules. At each interval one member receives the 'payout', the total amount collected from all members during that interval. Payouts are also called 'turns'.	*Variations on who receives the payout and when* Bidding clubs – these clubs offer members the opportunity to bid for an early turn in the rotation where the member winning the bid receives their payout first, but they pay extra throughout the cycle for the privilege of having gone first.
	The contributions for each interval can either be the same (e.g. $100) or different. Differing amounts are often called 'hands', 'shares', or 'throws'. One member may have one share, throw, or hand valued at $100. She would contribute $100 during each interval. Another member may have three. He would contribute $300 at each interval. When it is time to receive their payouts, assuming there are 10 people in the club, the first member receives $1000 and the second receives $3000.	Lottery clubs – Members claim their payouts randomly, not according to a schedule. They draw straws for who receives a payout during a particular interval. *Variations in contribution amounts* Some clubs allow 'share splitting' where two members cannot afford the minimum contribution so the members form a simple partnership. If the minimum share or hand is valued at $100, meaning a club member must contribute $100 per meeting, then each member contributes $50. They also split the payout.
	Each club determines the 'rotation schedule', meaning when each member is scheduled to receive their payout. When all members have received their payouts the 'cycle' or the 'rotation' ends. The club then can dissolve, start anew with the same members, or add and subtract members, depending on the club rules.	

(Continued)

Table 1 Continued

Club type	Basic functions	Variations
Insurance clubs	Members contribute the same amount for each beneficiary and cash in when an insured member of the family passes away. We call these contributions 'dues'. Beneficiaries typically include spouses or children. For example, if a member's spouse passes away and is registered as a beneficiary, the member receives financial (and often social) support from the club. If the member passes away, their beneficiary(ies) may receive financial support needed to bury the member.	*Variations on contributing to the insurance club* Typically, members contribute in advance a specified amount for each beneficiary and the money accumulates with the club until a member passes away. But some clubs gather in their contributions the moment a member passes and then funnel those funds to the beneficiary. *Variations on claiming funds once a member passes* Typically, the amount a beneficiary receives is fixed and based on the contributions of club members. However, some clubs decide how much a beneficiary receives based on need, not on the contribution made to the club by its member.
Savings and loan clubs	Members contribute sums of money at regular intervals (weekly, bi-weekly, monthly) to the club. We call these contributions, 'deposits'. The money accumulates. Members then lend money to other members according to club rules. The club sets the terms of the loan, the interest rate, and other rules. Some clubs will only lend for specific purposes (household emergencies; business improvement; etc.). Others let members borrow for any reason.	*Variations on contributions to the club coffers* Some clubs require equal deposits of all members at each interval. For example, every member must deposit $100 month. Other clubs allow members to deposit different amounts through a 'share' system. For example, one member might want to buy one share at $100 a month. Or another might want to buy three shares totalling $300 a month. If and when the club dissolves its funds, each member receives principal and interest according to the shares they held.

CHAPTER 1
The social life of money

Creating wealth: The alchemy of money clubs

In 2005, we (Jeff and Kim, the co-authors of this book) noticed something happening in our classrooms. Each of us was teaching at a major American university. In fact, Jeff was teaching at two – Columbia and Brandeis – while Kim taught at Tufts. Let us place a hold on the classroom discovery by disclosing a bit of background first.

Before teaching, we had worked together for years as colleagues in the US and abroad and were accustomed to sharing ideas. Some of our exchanges centred on how to improve microfinance institutions that lent to the poor. Other conversations focused on how to reach the most remote, excluded, destitute women with useful financial services. But, what indeed was useful to women who had only a few coins to spare? After years of working at field sites in the US, Africa, Asia, and Latin America, we saw that some microlenders or microfinanciers behaved like consumer lenders in the US. They charged exorbitant rates of interest and shook down their debtors in ways that resembled back alley loan sharks.

Equally disturbing was that if microfinance institutions – organizations that generally lent money to groups of low-income women – didn't do the dirty work of collecting late payments directly, they could encourage women in their loan groups to do it for them. Women's loan groups were the guarantors of borrowers in their same group. If one woman were late in her repayment, her fellow group members were responsible; they would need to make good on the delayed payment to the microlender. At first, the group might nudge the tardy woman to repay or in many cases even pay for her, but later, if the money was still overdue, the group might take action. That could mean seizing her goat, removing her from the groups, or shaming her in front of fellow worshipers at the temple, church, or mosque.

Around the time when numerous microfinance practitioners, including us, were growing disenchanted with the field, hopeful developments emerged in places like India and Niger. In these locations, groups of women were coming together to pool their own funds, often with the help of an NGO organizer. These methods were generically known as savings groups. Instead of a financial institution making the loans, the groups mobilized their own funds that they lent to members.

Though money in their villages was scarce, most people could usually muster something to put in a communal pot. The group then would decide who might receive a first loan from the fund. It could be someone in need of food or medicine or someone who wanted to buy a chicken. The group also decided the terms of the loan and the rate of interest. As loans were issued and repaid, the fund would grow and, as it did, larger loans could be disbursed. Since members were neighbours and knew each other well vetting new members was easy. Sure, there might be a time when a member had difficulty repaying a loan, but the group would know whether bad luck had befallen her – in which case they would step in to help – or whether she was unwilling to pay. The latter instances happened infrequently, for the character of each member was known through the everyday interactions that shape a neighbourhood or a village.

This form of microfinance was much gentler than its predecessor (loans from a microfinance institution), plus it had the advantage of keeping money in the community, not funnelled into the hands of usurious financiers. Recall that most microlenders were charging at minimum 24 per cent per year and some well over 100 per cent per year. Jeff remembers a time when he was in Cambodia. He had returned to that country after visiting it a year earlier to introduce the savings group method. When he inquired how the savings groups were doing, the villagers drew pictures with great gusto that showed group members chasing pricey lenders riding into the village on motorcycles right back out of the village. They were putting their own resources to use now.

Jeff and Kim began teaching graduate students at Columbia, Brandeis, and Tufts at about the same time as this new conception of microfinance – one premised on the pooled funds of locals versus the outside loans of microfinance institutions – was taking root. We were eager to teach our students about this exciting, expanding phenomenon.

Before we could bring the pooled fund or savings group concept into the classroom, we knew we would have to discuss more familiar approaches that students might have heard of. We took them through not only the storied Grameen Bank that famously lent small amounts of money to poor women in rural Bangladesh, with comparatively low interest rates, but also through the scandals that plagued SKS Microfinance in India, burdening borrowers by over-lending to them, while signalling to shareholders before an impending IPO (initial public offering) that the double bottom line was real: one could do well by doing good. But then came the problem from hell. A number of farmers indebted to SKS and similar lenders committed suicide on India's Deccan Plateau, near the city of Hyderabad. It seemed as if shareholders had to choose – do well or do good.

By the time we introduced students to the idea of local people forming a club and collecting and redistributing funds to club members, they were ready for it. To initiate our conversation, we took them on a tour of financial customs from around the world, which included investigating traditional systems of gathering and disbursing money. Kim would relay the story of a poetic villager in West Bengal, where she lived. He described his rotating club as a chariot's wheel. Powered by the pull of member aspirations, the wheel would rotate from the hands of one member to the next. When each had partaken in the wheel's munificence, it would cease its turning.

The mere mention of rotating clubs never failed to animate our international students. At least one and usually many more would have a friend, colleague, relative, or neighbour who had participated in such a club. Some students themselves had participated. Not only did club members use them to accumulate small sums of money, but also in many cases, they had saved large blocks of cash, enough to fund their graduate school tuitions.

Students would go on to describe how their parents pressed these clubs into service. They had secured the down payment for a mortgage through a rotating club, or had funded the purchase of vehicles or increases in their business inventory. Parents did this abroad in their home countries but also in the US.

Their rotating clubs all worked in similar ways regardless of where they were. Ten to twenty members, sometimes many more, would come together each week or month. During a meeting – often held under a mango tree, in a school room, or at the home of a member who had a comfortable house or porch – each would contribute the same amount to a common pot. At the end of the gathering, one club member would take the entire pot home. This would go on until all members had received the pot. The ultimate meeting, the one in which the last member received their payout, marked the end of a cycle at which point the club could either dissolve or begin afresh in a new cycle. Most groups continued cycle after cycle sometimes with one or two new members joining and one or two old members leaving.

Students claimed that in such clubs their parents benefited from saving (getting the pot at the end of a cycle) and borrowing (getting the pot at the beginning of the cycle). While technically their parents could have saved the same amount in a cash box in their homes or in a bank account, day-to-day demands could easily erode those sums. A child might want a new pair of shoes. An adult might want to upgrade her smartphone. A cousin, not for the first time, could ask for help with rent. Getting money out of the house and away from the needy hands of friends and relatives (and selves) gave club members an honest excuse for not coughing up the cash: 'I don't have any money on hand' proved a truthful reply to requests made by kith and kin. By participating in a rotating money club, members could be sure they were saving towards a goal. The club extracted savings from the hands of its members, placed them into the club's coffers, and then redistributed them as payouts. As each member claimed their share of the pot, their payout symbolized both their individual accomplishment and collective pride. The process had an alchemical quality to it: small sums of cash – when combined with discipline, mutual support, and patience – could be transformed into a car, a downpayment, or a small business.

The club as an idea, much like a Swiss army knife, could press into service various tools for objectives beyond money rotation. Throughout this book, it becomes evident that while rotating clubs, such as those just described, were prevalent, members also diversified and expanded their financial activities within the clubs. These included extending loans to fellow members in times of emergency or to support business ventures, as well as providing insurance coverage for themselves or their loved ones, primarily for funeral expenses.

First, some history

The three kinds of money clubs described – rotating clubs, savings and loan clubs, and insurance clubs – are rooted in traditions that span centuries. Communal forms of gathering money from individuals and then redistributing those funds to help people smooth their cash flow, expand their enterprises, and mitigate the shock of a death or medical emergency are not new. And over the centuries, these efforts have crystallized into the more formal or regulated structures that we enjoy today in the form of banks, insurance companies, and venture capital funds.

Governed by tradition as well as a sense of duty, historic money clubs filled crucial economic and social niches that neither commerce nor religion nor the simple fellowship of neighbours independently could provide.

Echoes of antiquity: Ancient wisdom in modern times

Money clubs of various kinds can trace their roots to the mutual aid societies of antiquity. In Ancient Egypt such were formed by stone cutters and in Ancient Rome by bricklayers. In the Middle Ages, Europe had similar clubs among members of guilds, themselves organized by craft or trade. The purpose of these clubs was to serve the families of guild participants, whose members included the ill and disabled, widows and orphans, those who had been befallen by harm, or any families who had suffered the loss of a breadwinner.[1]

At about the same time these guilds of the Middle Ages began to burgeon, money clubs proliferated in other parts of the world. For example, the *mujin* in Japan evolved from practices based on Buddhist traditions in India, China, and Korea. In the Muromachi period (1138–1467), the process of rotation, which we discuss in depth throughout this book, worked like most of the clubs we observed here in the US, with each member making periodic contributions and one member taking the entire sum home. In some *mujins*, members bid for their turn to take the pot home; in others, members drew lots to determine their turn. These two variations – bidding clubs and lottery clubs – also showed up in the clubs we observed.[2]

American clubs pre- and post-Civil War

While our field research in the US underscores that these clubs are part of an immigrant's story, history reveals that similar organizations flourished here as early as the 18th century.

Before 1865, both free and enslaved African Americans were actively engaged in economic empowerment efforts. They established numerous community organizations that prioritized mutual aid and savings. Similar to the rotating clubs found in West Africa, such as *esusu*, *susu*, partner, box-hand, *san*, or *tontine*, these clubs operated on principles of cooperation, trust, and mutual support.

Within these clubs, which operated in similar ways to other money clubs described in this book, members contributed agreed-upon sums to a common fund, from which funds were withdrawn according to a predetermined rotation. These funds served various purposes, including purchasing the freedom of relatives or even themselves from slavery, as well as facilitating economic advancement after emancipation.[3]

For example, in 1787, two prominent Black ministers founded the Free African Society in Philadelphia. Its mission was to foster mutual aid among members. The society, operating like a savings and loan club, not only aided the sick, widowed, and orphaned within Philadelphia's Black community but also extended its support to the broader city populace. It had a charitable component as well. One of its significant acts was the assistance it offered during the yellow fever outbreak of 1793, which claimed the lives of thousands of Philadelphians.[4]

Not all societies included a Black or African American membership. Many were started by and dedicated to white men and women. Perhaps the most famous was the Tontine Coffee House, serving both as a meeting place as well as a place to trade stocks, making it in 1793 the first indoor home of the New York Stock Exchange.[5] Membership in the *tontine* meant making investments in a life insurance plan that benefited the children of the coffee house's investors. Taking its name from the Neapolitan banker Lorenzo de Tonti who developed a financial scheme introduced in France in 1653, the *tontine* concept in countries colonized by the French has since evolved to include the rotating clubs referenced throughout this book.[6]

Beyond simple money clubs: The integral role of insurance in early American clubs

Distinguished by various names such as benevolent societies, fraternal orders, brotherhoods, and lodges, money clubs like the one just referenced functioned both openly and secretly. Their purpose was to pool funds to help those in need or in want of a better life. Insurance was often the motivating service. Mostly, clubs would pay the funeral costs of dues-paying members or their beneficiaries.

While many such societies served a local membership, at least one exception transcended geographical boundaries. The United Brothers of Friendship, originating in Kentucky in 1861 as a benevolent society – a type of insurance club – catered to both freemen and enslaved people. Evolving into a secret fraternity, in 1876 it amalgamated with the Sisters of the Mysterious Ten, an insurance club, establishing a female temple within its ranks. By 1878, the society had formalized its insurance services and transitioned from informal, pass-the-hat systems to written policies and structured claims.

With the incorporation of numerous local lodges, the organization rapidly expanded, attracting a membership of 60,000 individuals across the United States, Canada, Liberia, and the West Indies. Records from an annual session in 1913, overseen by officers bearing titles such as Grand Master and Grand Princess, highlight strict adherence to organizational by-laws alongside a celebration of music and prayer.[7]

W.E.B. Du Bois, a distinguished African American historian, chronicles in detail the proliferation and growing sophistication of these societies.

> There is probably no city in the land where there are as many societies among the colored people as in Baltimore, and several of the large societies which have spread far and wide, north and south, had their origin here. Nearly all of the societies are beneficial, but they may be divided in general into two classes, those beneficial merely and those with secret features. In order to help one another in sickness and provide for decent burial, through a system of small but regular payments, beneficial societies were formed among little groups of acquaintances or fellow laborers. In Baltimore they

date back to 1820, and were afterwards specially exempted from the state laws forbidding meetings of colored people. Twenty-five, at least, had been formed before the war ; from 1865 to 1870, seventeen or more were formed ; since 1870, twenty or more have been added, several as late as 1884 and 1885. The number of members vary from a dozen to over 100 [...]

These societies vary somewhat in details. The usual fees from members are 50 cents a month; the usual benefits are $4 a week for a number of weeks, and then reduced sums, in sickness, and $4,000 for death benefit. Some pay as long as sickness lasts. Some give widow's dues according to need. One, for example, the Friendly Beneficial Society, organized chiefly by the members of a Baptist church, some fifteen years ago, with the usual fees and benefits, carries a standing fund of about $1,000, and the yearly fees of the members have paid the current expenses of $300 to $500, and has usually allowed an annual dividend of $5 to each (Du Bois, 1907: 93–94).[8]

These benevolent societies closely resemble many insurance clubs discussed in this book. We encountered them not only operating in conjunction with rotating clubs but also independently. Contemporary clubs in the US adhere to the traditional burial society models of their homeland, integrating here and there contemporary communication technology for messaging and record-keeping. Their operations are similar to one another as well as to the benevolent societies just discussed: members paid monthly dues for themselves or their family members, typically spouses. It was common for members to wait at least three months before becoming eligible to make a claim. One club learned this lesson the hard way when a member immediately claimed to be dying of cancer upon joining, prompting the burial club to amend its by-laws to prevent such situations in the future.

Borrowing as another benefit, then and now

Benevolent societies in the 19th century offered more than insurance. Many were savings and loan clubs. Members could borrow for various purposes, such as medical expenses, funeral costs, education, or starting a business. These loans typically were offered at favourable terms with minimal interest rates, making them accessible to those who did not have access to conventional banking institutions. Often these societies birthed banks to specialize in financial services. One such spawn of a benevolent society was the St. Luke Penny Savings Bank, whose founder, Maggie Walker, herself the daughter of a former enslaved person, was determined to metamorphose pennies into dollars. The society, the Independent Order of St. Luke, had been her launch pad. In the late 1800s, she took the reins from an ineffective leader, and once she turned it into a sustainable institution, she set about setting up an independent bank dedicated to capturing savings and lending out deposits to local entrepreneurs.[9]

Although most contemporary clubs we encountered in the US weren't sizeable enough to initiate a bank, as in the instance above, we discovered one striving to do so. A Boston-based Bangladeshi club pools together US$96,000 monthly. Two members each receiving a $48,000 payout, deploy their funds towards entrepreneurial pursuits. While these amounts are significant, they fall short of elevating investments to levels needed for business acquisition or expansion. Despite actively pursuing bank financing to no avail, the club is now considering launching its own bank or credit union. In the meantime, members combine payouts to co-invest, typically in convenience stores in Boston's neighbourhood, Dorchester.

Hard-won discoveries: Students on research duty

We decided to learn how money clubs in the United States worked. Did they differ from immigrant culture to immigrant culture? Were they used primarily for enterprise investment, household emergencies, or something in between? Did they include members of different genders, ages, languages, or immigrant groups? How did they arrive at club rules, recruit new members, and support them?

To undertake such a study, we believed we would do well to recruit our graduate students to become researchers. We would focus on those who had native-level proficiency in the mother tongue of the immigrant group. Ideally, they would not only speak the relevant language, but they would also demonstrate two more qualities. First, they had to have the persistence to locate their interviewees, and second, they had to be curious. If they were not persistent, finding immigrants willing to chat about their money clubs would be impossible. And, if they were incurious, the immigrants would sense 'the homework assignment' aspect of their endeavours and disclose as little as possible. For immigrants to divulge the inner workings of their private clubs, conversations had to be shot through with a student's sense of wonder. Only then could they entice their subjects to reveal what they might ordinarily prefer to conceal.

Our researchers went to great lengths to find interviewees. Indeed, that was the most challenging part of their task. Some found willing participants through community organizations, others in restaurants, and still others at taxi stands and airports. One of Jeff's students paced the bustling streets of Queens, New York, dragooning whomever she could into talking with her. But when at last she had corralled a willing club member, a magical world opened up to her. She was treated to the food, language, and music of a place she longed for – Bangladesh. 'Almost as soon as I stepped out of the rickety New York City 'E' train at the Jackson Heights/Roosevelt Ave stop in Queens, I breathed in the welcoming, familiar, and pungent scents of home – a fusion of incense, milky tea, and spices.' That was just the beginning of her discovery.

Club members willing to talk responded that they enjoyed teaching a younger generation about the traditions that got them to where they were. Speaking the language, and sharing music and meals was fun for interviewees, too. But, not all student researchers shared the kind of heritage that drew club members close to our researchers. Kim had two American students who had language proficiency in the immigrant's spoken tongue but did not possess the level of insider knowledge that accompanies one who has grown up within the norms of a particular culture, such as the Bangladeshi one just mentioned.

The American students struggled and entertained more than a few misadventures in the process. Still, they managed to find humour in adversity. For example, one travelled from Boston to New York to meet with two Egyptian guards at the Metropolitan Museum of Art. Aaron, the student, had been referred to the guards by friends back in Egypt. When he dutifully showed the guards the paperwork needed to comply with Tufts' ethical board, they ran off never to be seen again. (Note: the paperwork is extensive and possibly designed to scare off anyone. Lesson: complete it later out of view of the research subject.) Dejected, Aaron headed back to

Boston and once in town stopped for a meal at a local eatery. He was hungry and on edge. While standing in line awaiting his order, he and a young Haitian man exchanged a few friendly remarks. When Aaron shared his story of the failed interview, the Haitian exclaimed, 'I belong to a club just like that. You can interview me!' And so Aaron did. That story appears in the case called, 'Mama Sol and Papa Sol'.

Despite the obstacles encountered by both international and American students, our researchers persevered, learned, and then shared their lessons. They enjoyed, or so they told us, discoveries about their own cultures or new cultures, and delighted in the small ironies and many serendipities that make field research so unpredictable and so rewarding.

This book is the culmination of our studies. We are pleased to share with readers the determination, discipline, and resourcefulness that characterize these clubs as they cement social bonds and drive members towards their singular purpose of prosperity and their plural vision of the American Dream.

Folk banking: The diaspora and their money clubs

The American Dream of earning a good living, buying a home, sending children to school, and building a life regardless of social stature or place of birth is an aspiration for many who immigrate to the US.[10] While new immigrants may be fleeing 'push factors' of violence, poverty, and persecution, they are also 'pulled' by the prospects of a better life for themselves and their children.

Some arrive in the US wealthy,[11] educated,[12] and fluent in English.[13] Many of the cases in this book, however, focus on immigrants who may arrive with just a few dollars in their pocket, may struggle with English, and may lack legal status, if only temporarily. These new arrivals mostly work in low-paying jobs in construction, dishwashing, cooking, domestic cleaning, and day care, with many earning an income – at least initially – in the shops of immigrants from their home countries.[14] Households often weave together a living from multiple jobs performed by several family members. Income fluctuates from week to week and season to season. Expenses, our interviewees told us, can be just as unpredictable as their income. Health care, car repairs, rent, death, or an illness will almost certainly occur, and without financial buffers in place, these costs could set families back substantially. But we also include cases where immigrants have built profitable businesses for themselves and are living comfortable, middle-class lives in the US, often with the help of their various kinds of money club.

In this book, we discuss several kinds of clubs: rotating clubs, burial or insurance clubs, and savings and loan clubs. The most common and the workhorse of amassing funds is the rotating club. Since most of the clubs in this book address rotating clubs, we'll discuss lending and insurance clubs first.

Savings and loan clubs – borrowing from pooled funds

We encountered clubs where members deposited money into a common fund and allowed that fund to grow. We observed that the primary reason for joining a savings and loan club was to borrow from it. It was common for them to spring up alongside a rotating club and include the same members.

In Asheville, North Carolina, for instance, members of a rotating club were also engaged in a *caja de ahorro* (savings box), their term for a savings and loan club. As with their rotating club, members of the *caja de ahorro* regularly contributed specified sums of money which they called deposits. However, instead of distributing these deposits as payouts according to a rotation schedule, the money in the savings and loan club accrued. Members applied for loans and repaid the principal and interest according to club rules.

Interest rates in savings and loan clubs varied but generally hovered around 10 per cent monthly. Some distributed the accumulated deposits – interest and principal – back to individual members after a set period, while others distributed interest only. The principal, untouched and allowed to grow, generated dividends in the form of interest and of course loan capital for members. These clubs often imposed borrowing limits based on a multiple of a member's deposits into the club's fund. For instance, if a member had deposited $100 into the savings and loan club, they could borrow up to $300, with their deposits serving as partial loan collateral.

Methods for collecting funds in savings and loan clubs were diverse. In Seattle, Ethiopian members not only made regular contributions to their rotating club but also made an additional deposit of $20 to a separate savings and loan club, whose coffers took the form of a lockbox. The recipient of the rotating club payout would safeguard the contents of the lockbox until the next meeting when the box was handed over to the new payout recipient. At the meetings, the secretary counted the contents of the lockbox in full view of the members, while the designated bookkeeper recorded the amounts in a ledger.

We observed other ways of collecting funds as well. For example, a Tanzanian rotating club, called an *upato*, held a Wakanda event on one Valentine's Day. The party was themed on the fictional home of the superhero Black Panther and proved to be a great fundraiser. They turned their $10,000 proceeds into a savings and loan club, its membership identical to that of the *upato*. A member could borrow a maximum of $2,000 at 10 per cent monthly interest. Members made monthly deposits directly into the savings and loan club's bank account. While the account was managed by the chairperson and the secretary, the information was available to any member. The savings and loan club continued to collect deposits, but when we last interviewed the secretary, the club had been facing challenges:

> We started with very high spirits, but now we are struggling with the monthly deposits. On the 25th of last month, we set a deadline for all remaining loans to be settled. We wanted to distribute funds back to members. Every member in the group owes some money and we set a deadline so that everyone would clear their balances, but until now we haven't received anything – their other expenses are taking priority.

Insurance clubs – protecting members from a surge in expenses

Another common type of club we encountered was the insurance club, often called a burial club. Resembling the burial associations that flourished in the period before the American Civil War and well after in the United States, these clubs had the distinct markings of the members' country of origin.

Insurance clubs often collect dues monthly or annually. Upon a member's death or the death of their beneficiary, the club distributes funds to cover the costs of a funeral. An Ethiopian club in Boston, known as an *iddir*, comprises 100 Boston cab drivers. Registered as a non-profit organization, the club collects $30 monthly from each member, or $36,000 annually. The *iddir* not only covers funeral expenses for family members in Boston or Ethiopia but also contributes to the costs of transporting the deceased and two family members back to Ethiopia should they pass away in Boston.

In the event of a member's death, the *iddir* plays a pivotal role in coordinating all tasks related to the *lekso* (mourning customs) and funeral arrangements. Immediately after a death, the executive committee allocates various tasks among group members, including coordinating with the funeral home and arranging for the transport of the body. During the *lekso*, group members take charge of distributing bread and drinks to attendees, with taxi drivers' wives (the majority of the association's members are men) expected to assist with food preparation for the *lekso* and funeral lunches. At the funeral, *iddir* members often serve as pallbearers.

Also in Boston, the club of Tanzanians mentioned above operates their rotating club, their savings and loan club as well as their insurance club, with systems that differ somewhat from the *iddir* just described. Members make sure that $15,000 is always on hand in the club's bank account to front the needed funds. One member says,

> You have to be in the US to join, but after becoming a member, you can go anywhere in the world. The $15,000 will follow you as long as you're maintaining your membership by paying $20 at the beginning of the year and contributing to each death. We have had two deaths in Tanzania of members who had moved back home from the US. Both members received the full insurance amount because we could confirm that they were active members.

Rotating clubs: Engines of progress

Rotating clubs in other countries have been well-documented by scholars from around the world.[15] Researchers find similar patterns in their mechanics but with distinctive elements marked by cultural traditions.[16] The international roots of these clubs matter because clubs in the US generally adhere to practices honed in their ancestral homes.

Despite their new, American context, members reassured us that their club traditions – the *tanda* of Mexico, the *dhikuti* of Nepal, the *tontine* of Cambodia and West Africa, the *sol* or *sangue* of Haiti, the *pardner* of Jamaica, the *sou-sou* of Barbados, the *chama* of Kenya, the 'committee' of Pakistan, the 'association' of Côte d'Ivoire, the *shamiti* of Bangladesh, the *equob* of Ethiopia – were mostly flourishing here in the US.

While members originated from diverse corners of the world, their processes showed striking similarities. Regular contributions to the club's coffers yielded substantial payouts, offering members the flexibility to save up money, remit funds to their home countries, or invest in profitable ventures. Embedded within these clubs were the core principles of accountability, discipline, and mutual support reflective of the values necessary to a club's success. While the origins of each club may have incubated for decades in different locales around the world, the goal governing US rotating clubs is largely the same – members worked together so that each member could amass money in the presence of others that might otherwise be challenging to amass individually.

In the US, club members contribute fixed amounts of money over a predetermined period at regular intervals. Members rotate who receives the pooled contributions, referred to as a 'pot' or payout. For instance, a club might require each member to contribute $200 weekly for 10 weeks, resulting in a $2,000 payout for one member each week for 10 weeks until all members have received their payouts.

Our research shows that informal savings practices are particularly prevalent among newly arrived immigrants, who leverage local networks in the US as well as in their countries of origin. Many members, as diaspora, direct their club payouts towards investments in properties or businesses back home, using transcontinental networks as a way to manage their wealth.

Our study is not the first to find relationships between financial networks and the diaspora. Many scholars have preceded us (Millman, 1997).[17] For instance, noted social anthropologist Michel Laguerre observed that New York-based members of rotating clubs, what he calls folk banking, directed payouts towards Haitian land and businesses, which ranged from warehouses to transportation infrastructure for agricultural goods (Laguerre, 1998).[18] We observed the same phenomenon: diverse diasporic communities in the United States, such as Kenyans in New Hampshire and Mexicans and Nepalis in the US northeast, channelled their payouts towards investments in their respective home countries, be they real estate or business ventures.

Today, some rotating clubs offer members the opportunity to bid for their placement within the rotation. For example, if the monthly contribution is set at $1,000 per member and there are 10 members in the club, each would typically receive a payout of $10,000. However, if a member draws a placement at the end of the cycle and wishes to expedite their payout, by contributing more than the nominal amount, they can bid for an earlier position. For instance, by agreeing to contribute $1,050 – $50 higher than the nominal contribution – they can secure the first position by outbidding others. Yet, should another member bid higher, say $75, they would then take the first position. The initial $50 bidder would then move to second position. Members perceive this as equitable, recognizing that later payout placements entail greater risk. The extra cash is distributed among the members at the end of the cycle.

In contrast to the predictability of a predetermined payout rotation, some clubs value the element of surprise. In New York, for instance, Bangladeshi *khelas* function akin to a lottery. Members make contributions every 15 days, mirroring a traditional rotating money club. However, the excitement lies in the uncertainty of who will receive the payout. Everyone looks forward to who will hold the winning straw at the meeting. By the cycle's end, every member is assured a payout. The thrill of a random draw serves as motivation for attendance. It is understood that if a member in need does not win the draw, the winner can opt to defer the payout to a later time, with the amount then going to the needy member.

A recent study in the US of 294 current or previous club members – 47 per cent male and 53 per cent female and 60 per cent earning less than $40,000 annually – shows similar findings (Ibrahim, 2020). The data show the propensity of participants to direct payouts – ranging between $1,000 and $5,000 towards major purchases or long-term investments. More than 28 per cent of participants used payouts for car purchases, closely followed by investments in small businesses (22.1 per cent). Other uses included home purchases (7.8 per cent), home repairs (7.5 per cent), and jewellery purchases (8.5 per cent). While the primary motivation for joining a money club was to achieve a goal, a substantial portion of payouts – more than 30 per cent – were used for emergency expenses. As we found in our research, participants directed payouts towards investments in their countries of origin, including small businesses, homes, land, or farms.

To gauge the impact of rotating club participation on asset ownership, this same study queried participants about their holdings before and after receiving a payout. The findings illustrate a significant increase in asset ownership post-payout across various categories. For instance, home ownership surged from 8.5 per cent to 22.1 per cent, and small business ownership also rose from 8.8 per cent to 25.2 per cent. Ownership of taxicabs and commercial trucks increased from 2.4 per cent to 7.1 per cent.

Behind closed doors: The inner workings of rotating clubs

Membership dynamics: Varied rules and motivations within clubs

One might expect that club members would come from different socio-economic backgrounds. And in many instances that is true. But in others, wealthier members make regular, sizeable contributions to the tune of hundreds and thousands of dollars but will allow financially struggling members to participate by splitting their contributions. If a nominal contribution is $500, then two members can team up to contribute $250 each, or much wealthier members can double or triple their regular contributions. (We address how multiple and split shares affect payouts later.) Such rules permit clubs to preserve solidarity within an immigrant community by adjusting contributions to the economic realities of their membership.

Some clubs exercise strict rules about who can be a member, often dictating age, gender, or country of origin as criteria. A club headquartered in Washington, DC specifies that members may be only of Ivorian descent or married to someone who is. The same is true for a club of women and men made up of Tanzanians and their spouses. Some clubs are even stricter. A club of Ethiopians in Boston states in its by-laws that members may only be Ethiopian cab drivers.

But many clubs are more inclusive, for example, a rotating club of women in Massachusetts has members originally from Guyana, Trinidad, Dominica, and several African countries. In Ashville, North Carolina, one club comprised members from the Mexican, Salvadorean, and Colombian populations.

Religion and caste can prove important when considering who can join. A club of Kenyans in New Hampshire counts only Christians among its membership. Just the opposite is true for a lottery club in New York. Its membership of 42 includes a mix of Bangladeshi Muslims and Hindus. While from similar socio-economic backgrounds – many members are small business owners – they believed in downplaying their religious affiliation in an effort to emphasize their identities as brothers and sisters in 'this land far from home'.

In contrast, Nepali clubs in New York mirror the social systems of their homeland. For them, trust comes with familiarity. Virtually all are from the same caste, religion, ethnic background, or region of Nepal. Some may have even come from the same village or family.

While we found members of most clubs located within meeting distance, we also found clubs that held together geographically distant members. For example, a Guatemalan club in Massachusetts has members located in the western part of the US; a Somali club in Boston is managed by a club member in Texas; and an Ivorian club has members scattered throughout the country. The willingness to keep far-flung members in the fold is based on the mutual trust members have earned either among themselves or with their organizers.

From do-it-yourself to professional: Diverse ways that clubs organize

In the case studies profiled here, group organizers explained how they select members, collect and distribute funds, and balance flexibility with stability in managing club mechanics. Organizers spoke at length about what motivated them to undertake the time-consuming and potentially financially risky task of managing their rotating clubs. Volunteer organizers highlighted the satisfaction this work provided them, and how the clubs supported entrepreneurship and filled an essential financial need for members.

Organizers are typically tasked with setting the rules for admission, collecting and distributing funds, and running meetings if the group meets in person, or communicating with the group remotely.

Some manage their rotating clubs as a socially beneficial exercise and value the respect of members who appreciate their time and effort. They in turn like the idea of supporting those in their care. 'Now that I have more security than when I arrived, I want to help people who are in the same situation I was in when I came to this country, and helping people save is a great way to do that'. Others came into the job because of the revered position their family holds in the eyes of the larger community; these organizers are seen as responsible and trustworthy. In both instances, organizers volunteer their time.

Many organizers receive a 'tip' when a member gets their payout. A 'tip' is a form of thanks and likely not enough income to fully compensate organizers for their time. As each member receives their payout, they give a sum to the organizer as compensation. According to our research, most paid organizers take small tips of between $30 and $100 within a single cycle.

In other instances, organizers manage their rotating clubs as a business, taking money beyond tips. As a financial incentive, some organizers receive the first payout of the rotation, effectively receiving an interest-free loan. Other organizers collect fees. One Nepali organizer in Queens, New York receives a combined $2,000 per month to manage two large *dhikutis*, one with 40 members and the other with 91 members. In other instances, organizers receive the first payout without having to contribute to the pot. Members are glad to compensate their organizers as they put great effort into making the club run smoothly and often guarantee payouts, meaning if one member fails to contribute, the organizer steps in to make the club whole.

Incentivizing participation: Payout as the driving force behind club membership

Payouts afford members a cushion of cash to help them pay rent, fix a broken car, buy appliances, or pay for a medical visit. As we see in this chapter, payouts can arrive unpredictably in cases where members prefer a lottery approach. But for those clubs that operate on a rotation schedule, members report that club payouts arrive predictably and lessen the need to take on debt or borrow from relatives or friends who themselves may be short of cash. They also said that as household income increases or becomes steadier, members can contribute more to their clubs. They either join clubs with larger contributions (and thus larger payouts) or purchase more than one 'hand' or share per meeting and receive double or triple the normal payout.

Larger payouts mean that members can fulfil their longer-term objectives, such as starting or expanding a business, building equity through a down payment on a home, or making investments both in the US and in their home country. It also means they can secure transportation by buying a car, which in turn can stabilize their incomes, either because members use their vehicles for business purposes, e.g. driving for Uber, or commute to better-paying jobs.

Cultivating trust: Time-honoured tactics

Trust was mentioned in every interview as *the* key to success. Members must trust that when it is their turn to receive the payout, all contributions will have arrived on time. For clubs with organizers, it is the organizers who carry the responsibility of managing collection activities and, in many instances, the organizer must guarantee on-time payment. It follows then that organizers maintain strict rules about who can join a rotating club and how to reduce the risk posed by its newest members. Often, rules dictate that new members are required to be relatives or workmates of other members. Even if not an explicit rule, the level of trust required often demands these kinds of close relationships, whether or not the club has an organizer.

New members are typically the last ones to receive their payouts. Their placement at the end of a rotation ensures they will keep contributing throughout. After a cycle or two and once proved trustworthy, they are permitted to take earlier positions, or 'numbers', in the next cycle.

However, we did find exceptions to the above. Members of a Nepali club in New York City worried that club rules were too strict to support new Nepali arrivals in the US. These young immigrants would need to pay rent, repay debts to those sponsoring their journeys, and, above and beyond these costs, contribute $1,000 a month to the club.

Compelled to find a 'pay-it-forward' solution, the club devised a plan. The immigrant's family or friends would sponsor them and make the first two contributions on their behalf. This gave the new member time to find a job while they secured a place to stay.

They might find work as a dishwasher at a Nepali eatery where they can earn $2,500 to $3,000 a month, working 10–12 hours a day, seven days a week. When the new member receives their payout at the first turn, they repay their families in Nepal who funded their travel to the US, with costs running between $15,000 and $68,000.[19] After the first two payouts in the cycle, the new member begins contributing to the club. They pay the $1,000 monthly contribution and an additional $30 or $40 per month in extra payments until the cycle is completed. Slowly over several cycles, the extra amounts contributed help pay down their loan to the sponsoring members.

We found no evidence to suggest that should a member miss a contribution the club would pursue the tardy payer legally. Clubs with organizers reported very few problems with contributions, indicating that those occur infrequently. They attributed the good performance to stringent vetting requirements. Members are scrutinized in different ways, at times by the organizer and at times by the members themselves. For instance, if a potential member is not familiar to the organizer or multiple current members, she may need to find at least one member willing to vouch for the potential member's character, and in some instances, the vouching member must guarantee the on-time contributions of the potential member, at least for the first cycle. Should the new member fail to contribute, the vouching member would then contribute for her.

And then, there is always social shame as a motivating factor. One friendly club of Bangladeshis in New York has taken shame to extremes. Attendance at the bimonthly meetings is mandatory; otherwise, members risk having their name posted by the club's secretary on the 'wall of delinquent shame'.

Capitalizing on opportunity: Business owners' increased investments and returns

In some cases, business owners form rotating clubs for the specific purpose of advancing their commercial interests. As membership matures and the size of contributions grows, club members can use payouts to purchase or start a business. For example, several Eritrean men in a Seattle rotating club used their payouts to purchase trucks for a transportation business. Five Kenyan club members in New Hampshire came together to start an adult day care business. In Queens, New York, Nepali immigrant members of a rotating club saw starting a business as the principal way to achieve 'the American Dream'. In their case, businesses included restaurants, eateries, local shops, and service businesses.

The Bangladeshi leader of a *shamiti* provided advice and assistance to peers starting or purchasing convenience stores. The payouts from his club, which were a substantial $48,000, became alternatives to high-interest loans that they would otherwise rely on for start-up funds. Sharing advice about staffing, financial management, and payroll automation, and sharing technology, is an integral part of a club's benefits.

While the above club has a sophisticated approach to investment – with payouts directed to investing in a branded chain of convenience stores – many smaller businesses brim in a ferment of entrepreneurship. For example, Nepali-run enterprises in New York include travel agencies, day care centres, churches, temples, restaurants, food carts, tax firms, law offices, taxi companies, newspapers, remittance centres, grocery stores, import/export shipment companies, printing firms, design agencies, clothing stores, fast-food processors, and more. *Dhikutis* have been their primary financial backers.

Balancing flexibility and structure: The not-so-immutable rules of money clubs

Members who urgently need money are often able to negotiate their placement in the payout cycle. Flexibility as a value also manifests itself in contributions and payouts. As we have noted already, those who can save more 'take two numbers' and receive twice the payout. Members who don't have enough income for the normal contribution can partner up with another, splitting both the payout and the contributions with their partner.

One Mexican organizer in New York prioritizes predictability above all else, enforcing *tanda* rules rigidly to produce her cherished predictability. 'Rules are rules,' she says. 'People have to respect the number they chose.' Members expressed profound reverence for the rules of their respective rotating clubs, understanding that participation could put their own finances as well as those of fellow members in peril.

Celebrate! How clubs bring more than money to their membership

Being part of a club offers rewards beyond the payout. We already discussed insurance, but some clubs go beyond the financial realm and bridge into the social. In these, members help each other with a death or illness in the family or for important events such as weddings and other social gatherings. In North Carolina, Mexican clubs plan for *quinceañeros*, special occasions to celebrate children's 15th birthdays. In Maine, Burundians found community and support from their clubs as they transitioned from Burundian norms to American culture and finance. An Ethiopian *Equob* in Seattle closes their meetings with a spread of snacks and a formal, traditional Ethiopian coffee hour.

The social aspect of money clubs falls on a spectrum whose endpoints are highly social and highly financial. The African, Latin American, and South Asian rotating club meetings may become social gatherings or occasions to participate in the same kinds of festival celebrated back in their home countries. In Queens, New York, Nepali immigrants join larger clubs where they contribute to celebrations or top up an emergency fund to help relatives back home. The same is true of Congolese immigrants living in New Hampshire.

Many clubs prize a good dinner or party as part of strengthening bonds among members. A large club comprising members hailing from Côte D'Ivoire in West Africa holds parties for members that can last till 3 a.m. Everyone looks forward to returning to the geographic origin of the club – Washington, DC; though many members have scattered to other regions of the US, they make the effort to come to the capital to enjoy an evening of festivities that follows the club's annual meeting.

Parties and gala events seemed part and parcel of Nepali and some Bangladeshi clubs in New York and Boston. In some instances, particularly in burial clubs, the club covers the costs of an annual gala event. In other instances, each member is expected to throw a party when it comes their turn to receive the payout.

Some respondents reported that their rotating clubs have a social fund. At each meeting, the club takes up a collection from members in addition to their regular rotating contributions. If a member or a relative back home dies or falls ill, an emergency fund will kick in to partially or fully cover expenses. Others fundraise to send money home as needed.

In other clubs, membership is viewed as a strictly financial arrangement. In these clubs, the organizer operates as a hub connecting member 'spokes'. Trust in the organizer is paramount to the sustainability of the club: members may lack close relationships with other members and in many instances don't know the identity of others.

Even in groups primarily comprising relatives and close friends, their rotating clubs may deal solely with financial matters, forgoing social or charitable activities. In these cases, members may voluntarily help one another but do so outside the bounds of their rotating club.

Hidden gems: The impact of rotating clubs in the US economy

The case studies in this book disclose how robust, informal financial networks thrive alongside but independently of the US formal financial system. This club-fuelled economy is invisible to outsiders. Time and again when the authors presented the club case studies to US regulators, banks, and non-profit executives, the audience expressed astonishment that these savings devices were operating under their noses. In Bloomington, Indiana, the staff of an agency focusing on housing did not know that the women she had been working with for years were part of a *tanda*.[20] The senior staff of a credit union in Albuquerque had no idea that most of their Latino staff was regularly saving in their rotating clubs.[21]

We could find no studies of savings and loan clubs nor insurance clubs, and struggled with uncovering evidence about rotating clubs. With rotating clubs so firmly hidden within the United States economy, uncovering their numbers is a challenge. However various studies point to how widespread the practice is. For example, a 2013 study of 443 Mexican, 417 Ecuadorian, and 464 Chinese immigrants carried out in New York City showed that 75 per cent of Mexicans and 69 per cent of Ecuadorans saved informally in rotating clubs.[22] Given that there are 40 million first-generation immigrants living in the United States, and if only a fraction saved money informally, their clubs could collectively save and distribute billions of dollars every year.

Estimations of the size of the rotating club sector can be tricky. Members may not admit to being part of a club. As a Haitian cab driver in Boston, Jean, told Kim, 'You can take my bank account, you can take my taxi, just don't take my *sol*. If the bank thinks I am in one *sol* [rotating club], and I am active in four [which he was], the government will pay me a visit. And that will be the end of my savings plan.' Jean was able to purchase a hackney licence for $250,000 and add two cars to his taxi fleet through a combination of leases and club payouts. Whether his fear of the United States Government stemmed from a real or imagined threat, Jean believed that 'Uncle Sam' would not hesitate to fine him or shutter his clubs altogether.

The apparent prevalence of rotating clubs, and their real – if difficult to measure – financial impacts warrant further attention from policymakers and the formalized financial sector. Jeff, using a combination of World Bank data combined with his own research, estimates that, in the US, these largely invisible money clubs mobilize and distribute close to $42 bn. However, the authors concur that accurately estimating the mobilization and distribution of money generated by these clubs, which operate discreetly, relies more on skilled reckoning than on precise calculation.

As the case studies show, these clubs have proven transformative for the lives and fortunes of immigrant communities in the United States. Thoughtful institutionalization of these clubs could not only better serve their members, but also the broader communities in which they live.

Notes

1. Archambault, E. (2010) 'Mutual Organizations/Mutual Societies', in H.K. Anheier and S. Toeplar (eds.), *International Encyclopedia of Civil Society*, Springer, New York NY.
2. Dekle, R. and Hamada, K. (1996) 'On the Role of Informal Finance in Japan, Its Prototype: Mujin (Rotating Finance) and its Public Substitute: The Postal Savings System', *The Center for Institutional Reform and the Informal Sector*. https://pdf.usaid.gov/pdf_docs/pnabx793.pdf
3. Josiah, B.P. (2004) 'Providing for the Future: The World of African American Depositors of Washington DC's Freedmen's Savings Bank, 1865–1874,' *The Journal of African American History* 89 (1): 1–16.
4. Yee, S. (2011) 'Free African Society of Philadelphia (1787–?)', *Blackpast*, February 10. https://www.blackpast.org/african-american-history/free-african-society-philadelphia-1787/

5. Nadine, M.A. (2002*) Confessions of a ... Coffee Bean: The Complete Guide to Coffee Cuisine.* Square One Publishers, Garden City NY.
6. Jennings, R.M. and Trout, A.P. (1976) 'The Tontine: Fact and Fiction,' *Journal of European Economic History* 5: 663–70.
7. Grand Temple of Kentucky (1913) *Proceedings of the Annual Session of the Grand Lodge: Annual Session of the Grand Temple of the United Brothers of Friendship, Sisters of the Mysterious Ten, P.M.C., R. H. and Juveniles of Kentucky*, Grand Lodge of Kentucky, Georgetown, KY.
8. Du Bois, W.E.B. (1907) Economic cooperation among negro Americans, a social study made by Atlanta University Under the Patronage of the Carnegie Institution of Washington, DC. The Atlanta University Press, Atlanta, GA.
9. McGrath, M. and Beale, M. (2012) 'Why America's First Black Female Bank Founder is Still Owed a Great Debt', Forbes, https://www.forbes.com/sites/maggiemcgrath/2021/03/20/why-americas-first-black-female-bank-founder-is-still-owed-a-great-debt/?sh=1e0e702c7fd3
10. *See* Cowell, S.R. (n.d.). 'Lesson Plan: The American Dream,' *Library of Congress*, retrieved November 22, 2022, from. https://www.loc.gov/classroom-materials/american-dream/#procedure
11. *See* Painter, M.A. and Qian, Z. (2016) 'Wealth Inequality among New Immigrants,' *Sociological Perspectives*, 59 (2): 368–394. http://www.jstor.org/stable/26339117
12. *See* Krogstad, J. and Radford, J. (2018) 'Education Levels of U.S. Immigrants are on the Rise,' *Pew Research Center*. Washington D.C. Retrieved from https://www.pewresearch.org/short-reads/2018/09/14/education-levels-of-u-s-immigrants-are-on-the-rise/
13. *See* Batalova, J., Hanna, M., &and Levesque, C. (2021) 'Frequently Requested Statistics on Immigrants and Immigration in the United States,' *Migration Policy Institute*. Retrieved November 22, 2022, from. https://www.migrationpolicy.org/article/frequently-requested-statistics-immigrants-and-immigration-united-states-2020
14. *See* Organisation for Economic Cooperation and Development. (n.d.) 'Demography and Population, Migration and Statistics, Immigrants by Sector,' *OECD Statistics*. Retrieved from https://stats.oecd.org/; *see also* Grieco, E. (2004) 'What Kind of Work Do Immigrants Do?', *Migration Policy Institute*. Retrieved November 22, 2022, from. https://www.migrationpolicy.org/research/what-kind-work-do-immigrants-do-occupation-and-industry-foreign-born-workers-united-states

15. Ardener, S. and Burman, S. (1995) *Money-Go-Rounds: The Importance of Rotating Savings and Credit Associations for Women*, BERG, Oxford U.K.
16. Adams, D.W. and Seibel, H.D. (2020) 'The Expanding World of Self-Help Financial Groups,' unpublished.
17. Laguerre, M.S. (1998) 'Rotating credit associations and the diasporic economy', Journal of Developmental Entrepreneurship 3(1): 23–34.
18. Laguerre, M.S. (1998) 'Rotating credit associations and the diasporic economy', Journal of Developmental Entrepreneurship 3(1): 23–34.
19. Sapkota, J. (2019) 'A Nepali Man's Odyssey from Dang to San Diego', *The Kathmandu* Post, https://kathmandupost.com/national/2019/06/29/a-nepali-mans-odyssey-from-dang-to-san-diego
20. Interviews carried out January 8–11, 2019, in Bloomington, Indiana, by Jeffrey Ashe.
21. Conversation with Eric Kinman, founder of Solidarity Foundation and cooperative expert, 2017.
22. *See* Gons, N. (2013) 'Immigrant Financial Services Study', *New York City Department of Consumer Affairs*. Retrieved January 9, 2022 from https://www1.nyc.gov/assets/dca/downloads/pdf/partners/Research-ImmigrantFinancialStudy-FullReport.pdf

CHAPTER 2
Case studies of clubs with Asian roots

Business and community building among Boston's Bangladeshi immigrants: *Shamitis* as social and financial networks

For Asif, a club is more than just a place to save money. The Bangladeshi shamiti *is a flexible, informal network that allows immigrants like himself to leverage their resources and build thriving businesses in Boston, Massachusetts. The author of this case is Pranab Banik, Jeff's former student.*

This case study explores how a 'turn *shamiti*', a type of Bangladeshi rotating club, meets the needs for finance, belongingness, and community for Bangladeshi immigrants.

As I learned about how the *shamitis* worked, I became intrigued by their simplicity and flexibility. As a microfinance expert who has worked for many years in Bangladesh for BRAC, one of Bangladesh's largest microfinance providers, I was amazed to see how these clubs managed risks, identified challenges, and found solutions without any outside support. It is as if they had replicated many of the benefits of the Bangladeshi microfinance model as a no-cost way to serve their needs. I was eager to learn more about how they worked.

At first, I found it difficult to find someone willing to talk with me, but then I met Morshed. Morshed, a member of such a club, became an important informant: sharing his own story and introducing me to others. Now, he is the sole owner of one convenience store, and part owner of five others, while also serving as the general secretary of the Convenience Store-Owners' Association of Boston. Morshed estimates that 40 per cent of the convenience stores in Greater Boston are owned by Bangladeshis, due in no small part to *shamiti* savings.

After telling me how the *shamitis* operated, Morshed introduced me to Asif.

Asif's story

Asif came to America 16 years ago, dreaming of a prosperous life in the United States. In his early years he felt isolated and disconnected. He worked seven days a week for years as an employee in a convenience store owned by someone else. He said, 'I worked extremely hard, but I was not able to enjoy the fruits of my labour'. Asif knew he could overcome his situation by launching a business of his own, but he couldn't raise the necessary start-up capital. 'This is not an individual issue. I have met several Bangladeshi immigrants interested in small businesses who are facing [similar] difficulties', he said. As he thought about a solution, he remembered how his uncle who lived in Bangladesh had organized a *shamiti* that made him 'a hero' in his business and community.

Asif remembered:

> One day when I went to meet my maternal uncle in his cloth store located at Mirpur, Dhaka, I was amazed to see 30 people gathered there that night. Each deposited 5,000 Bangladeshi takas with one of the members receiving a payout of 150,000 takas [about $1,800]. I learned that they were not only going for the chance of winning the payout but they also attended the meeting to discuss their businesses and even social issues. For example, during that same meeting, a businessman asked for help in finding an employee for his store. Immediately his problem was solved by another member willing to support him. The meeting ended with a tasty meal.

Asif saw that his uncle in Bangladesh was able to expand his business quickly. He wondered if a *shamiti* would also be beneficial for the Bangladeshis living in the Boston area. Like those who were members of his uncle's *shamiti*, many Bangladeshi immigrants in Boston owned small businesses or had plans to start one. Although they had similar needs, it was not easy for Asif to convince others like him to understand the benefits – people questioned the legality of *shamitis* in the US and feared that someone would disappear with the money after the first payout.

However, Asif persevered – going door to door to motivate others to join. With another Bangladeshi and former colleague, Asif recruited 19 other Bangladeshis to his *shamiti*. Most were friends and relatives who had known and trusted each other for a long time. The initial 19 members agreed to purchase 26 shares every month for 19 months. Each share was worth $1,000. Some agreed to purchase more than one share so their payout would be larger. For example, if one member purchased two shares each month, he would be contributing a monthly $2,000 to the *shamiti*. His payout would then be $38,000 instead of the $19,000 designated for one share. The members selected as their leader an older, trustworthy, and well-respected businessman in the community.

Both Asif and his partner were excited to see that after a few months, members had become optimistic about the club and confident about their futures. After the completion of the first cycle in 2017, Asif and his associates formed a new turn *shamiti* consisting of 48 members. They increased the value of each share from $1,000 to $2,000; the total contribution jumped to $96,000 per month. This amount was always split – two members received the $48,000 payout. To manage such a large club, Asif divided members into four groups of 12, each with a leader who managed the payments for his group, freeing Asif to work with just 4 members rather than 48.

While Asif used his payout to become a partner in a new business, he also acknowledged that he appreciated the non-monetary benefits of being part of a *shamiti*. For instance, he mentioned that the recurring problem of finding help to staff his business 'is no longer an issue' since members collectively find and lend employees to each other. He added that Bangladeshi immigrants have greatly benefited from the informal jobs emerging from the *shamiti*'s network of new friends. Asif reflected, 'for half a decade I worked hard for others in a convenience store with little pay and no prospect of moving upwards. My life was stressful'. He shared how grateful he was that his *shamiti* helped him enjoy the fruits of his labour.

Morshed's story

Building on the prior case, this update illuminates how an American twist on the shamiti *tradition can nurture business growth. The entrepreneurial nature of this case's* shamiti *raises not only the possibility, but explicit interest in, linking of this kind of club with formal financial institutions.*

The authors of this story are Pranab Blanik, Jeff's former student, and Annie Bright, Kim's former student. This update builds on the previous story about Asif, which was written in 2018. The following was written in 2023.

Morshed Humayun, a friend of Asif, the businessperson just profiled, is an entrepreneur from Bangladesh. Having lived in Massachusetts for nearly 25 years, he is an active member and leader within the Bangladeshi business community, which has streamlined traditional *shamitis*, rotating clubs, to create financial opportunities for Bangladeshi entrepreneurs in the US.

He is currently part of two separate clubs: one with Asif, where members, all business owners, have access to substantial payouts, and one for convenience store owners, the Boston Bangladeshi Business Association. In this case, we focus on the club for convenience store owners.

The club emerged in response to obstacles that Morshed and his colleagues experienced as business owners. They wanted to expand and improve operations but lacked the needed capital.

> To start a store, you need $200,000–$300,000. Nobody has that much cash on hand. Before our associations began, we would have to go to 'hard lenders' to start our businesses … interest rates would be 15–20 per cent a year. Two years ago, for example, one of our business groups went to a hard lender to take out a loan for $200,000 for a project we were doing in Lowell, Massachusetts.

When formal banks rejected their requests to borrow funds to invest in Boston businesses, the community decided to upgrade traditional *shamitis*, Bangladeshi rotating clubs, to create financial opportunities for entrepreneurs in the US.

The Boston Bangladeshi Business Association rotating club includes 50 accounts or shares, but only 35 members, thus some members own more than one share. Each account holder contributes $2,000 to the club pot. At the monthly meeting, the pot is distributed to two members. Each account, then, receives a payout of $50,000. The rotating club continues until all accounts have received a payout, at which point members may begin a new cycle.

Members – all owners of convenience stores – guarantee club payouts by pledging their businesses as collateral. 'This is a long-term commitment,' Morshed explained, 'so, the number one condition for this association is that you must have collateral. For us, this means you can't enter the club unless you have a store'. The high-stakes nature of this association – and of its shared liability – leads to very selective approaches to membership.

Morshed divided the 50 accounts into two groups, which he calls teams. Although the club is regulated informally, it does involve financial analysts, collateral, and evaluation of the cash flow of potential members. Three officers are responsible for each team: a president, a treasurer, and a secretary. When considering a new candidate for membership, the team analyses the individual and their assets. To join, members must show that their stores have a reliable, monthly cash flow. The stakes for admitting new members are high, given that the club is the participants' sole source of funding, and is grounded in a mutual, cultural understanding:

> We have our own version of [interest] 'rates' within our system. We are all Bangladeshi, so we all have a cultural understanding of how things work. That's why your relationships matter. That's why collateral matters. Even if someone had a billion dollars, we wouldn't just let them into our club. Because if we don't have close enough relationships with them, who would be willing to be held liable for them?

In any given month, payouts are distributed in two ways. The first payout follows an established order determined at the beginning of the cycle. The second payout is not regular, but based on a lottery system in which a winner is randomly chosen in a draw. Members like both the predictability of the first payout and the surprise of the second payout. By the end of the 25-month cycle, all accounts will have received both payouts.

Members invest their payouts in a range of projects including real estate and rental cars. The club itself has made 90 acquisitions in convenience stores, purchasing them in neighbourhoods that can generate good returns. Avoiding the high rents of downtown, the group has sought stores in Boston communities like Dorchester and Mattapan for their lower rents and high demand for convenience-goods. Because $50,000 is insufficient to purchase a convenience store, often members will co-invest with payout recipients to raise the total capital needed.

Morshed and his club members have been creative when it comes to leveraging low-cost support in service to their Boston stores. He notes that while all members plan to stay – and therefore invest – in property in the US rather than Bangladesh, many invest in human capital back home to maintain their businesses:

> I do have one small satellite office back home in Bangladesh that monitors all of our stores' camera systems. They do a great job. They alert us to someone hiding or stealing things, and they can call the Boston police from a US number to respond to an incident they see on camera.

They send Morshed reports and perform other services like payroll, inventory management, and employee monitoring. Others in the club similarly leverage connections back home to save money, noting that while some pay $500 monthly for payroll, employee monitoring, and store security, those using Bangladeshi services can pay as little as $80 a month.

Morshed has high hopes for the future. He and his fellow members hope to start or collaborate with a bank or credit union to increase their access to capital.

Savings and solidarity in the lottery – Bangladeshi *khelas* in New York City

A researcher finds that immigrants from her country of origin, Bangladesh, have put a new spin on rotating clubs: the thrill of surprise that comes from a random approach to winning a payout. This lottery model of payouts works in similar ways to the rotating model but leaves getting the pot to chance. Tasfia Zaman is a former student of both Jeff and Kim.

My first Bangladeshi friend after coming to New York was a man named Kamal who worked as a server at a fast-food store. Kamal went out of his way to assist in my research, feeling motivated that his efforts would help highlight the success of New York's Bangladeshi immigrants. Kamal introduced me to his manager, Tanhid Uncle ("uncles" is a term used for respected older men), who then introduced me to several of his Bangladeshi contacts in New York. He advised that I visit the borough of the Bronx as well as the neighbourhoods of Jackson Heights and Jamaica in the borough of Queens. He said that was where *ershamitis* were likely to flourish.

Almost as soon as I stepped out of the rickety New York City 'E' train at the Jackson Heights/Roosevelt Ave stop in Queens, I breathed in the welcoming, familiar, and pungent scents of home – a fusion of incense, milky tea, and spices. Many of the people waiting on the subway platform were dressed in traditional South Asian attire, wearing *salwar kameez*, *sari*, and *panjabi*.

Lottery-based rotating clubs

One afternoon, when I was frustrated by having spent the whole day with only one fruitless interview to show for my work, I noticed a group of uncles sitting together outside, laughing, chatting, and happily munching on salty, spiced cucumbers. I confidently approached them and explained my research project, which was to learn about customary ways that Bangladeshis pool their funds. They were impressed that I would care about these traditions and invited me to join a club meeting to observe the proceedings.

All my conversations were conducted in Bangla, peppered with a little English here and there. I assured participants that their respective identities would be protected. I simply wanted to understand the money management process of their rotating clubs and how they might be helping Bangladeshis get ahead in America. While discussing business investment clubs, I noticed an excited shift in their responses when I brought up the terms 'khela' and 'lottery'. They were very accustomed to this practice and happy to tell me how it worked.

The rotating clubs, in this case a *khela* (meaning 'game' in English), included 42 members and both Bangladeshi Muslims and Hindus from similar socio-economic backgrounds who had immigrated to the US from the 1980s and into the 2010s. Many were Uber drivers, restaurateurs, or small business owners. Interestingly, while Bangladesh is a Muslim-majority country, ethnic identity became the strongest identifier for the young men travelling alone from Bangladesh – becoming brothers in 'this land far from home' irrespective of religious identity. Additionally, the Hindus in the club were amenable to their Muslim brothers' desire to provide interest-free loans from their lottery winnings. Their sense of community and mutual respect kept the club going strong for nine years, with many more to follow.

In this specific lottery-based rotating club, members make their contributions every 15 days, which must be paid by 6 p.m. on meeting days. Attendance at the bimonthly meetings is mandatory; otherwise, members risk having their names posted by the club's secretary on the playfully dubbed 'wall of delinquent shame'. The *khela* cycle renews every two years after everyone has received their payout. New members may not join in the middle of a cycle.

Each member can hold anywhere between one and five lottery tickets. If they hold one lottery ticket, they contribute $200 to the community pot; if they hold two lottery tickets, they contribute $400, and so on. A member can increase his chances of having his name drawn from the lottery bowl if he holds more than one ticket. However, there is no guarantee his name will be chosen. Fortunately for those who urgently need the money, a lottery winner can transfer the payout to a friend who needs the money more than they do. At the end of the cycle, all will receive their individual payouts, depending on the initial amount they put in.

This method, albeit contradictory to the structure of most of the clubs described in this book, places more emphasis on the thrill of winning the lottery than on the predictability of receiving a payout on a given date. The total amount distributed every 15 days among four winners from the 42 members amounts to about $30,000. However, the total payout varies every month as members can choose to withdraw or add their names to the lottery draw.

To welcome me to their *khela*, members allowed me to draw the first ticket from the lottery bowl. When I read out the name on the ticket, the members collectively booed the winner since he was someone who didn't need the money; plenty of other members could have used it to pay for a new $20,000 taxi cab or put a down payment on their mortgage. I was then told that if the winner was feeling generous, he could transfer his payout to the member who desperately needed the funds. At the end of the *khela*, no cash is left on the table. All has been disbursed.

It was clear that no one was following a cookie-cutter plan for achieving prosperity. While respondents felt rewarded both monetarily and socially, they did face risks. After my interviews, I questioned the safety mechanisms in place to ensure that mishaps did not happen. I wondered, 'How much can you control and how much do you leave on trust? However we might answer that question, these lottery-style *khela*s have enabled members to realize their own American Dream, and gave me hope that future immigrants to the US can similarly find success.

Risk and reward in Cambodian *tontines*: A declining tradition in Lowell, Massachusetts

Participating in a tontine *can be a gamble – it can bring great success or misfortune depending on how members use their payouts. In anecdotes from Mrs. Sea, a rotating club member, and others, one sees how trust is integral to the operation of a bidding rotating club and how an older generation relies on this cornerstone system. Kimlay Lev, Jeff's former student, is the author of this story.*

To study the *tontine*, the Cambodian version of a rotating club, I needed access to the Cambodian community in Lowell, Massachusetts. My uncle, a Buddhist priest living in Lowell, provided exactly that; he gave me his connections and I took it from there.

Lowell may seem like an unexpected hub for Cambodians, but the community has roots that span three decades. Having received members of Cambodia's well-educated elite fleeing the Pol Pot regime in the late 1970s, Lowell became an attractive destination for a second wave of migration in the 1980s. With an existing Cambodian presence, an abundance of jobs for low-skilled labourers, refugee-friendly policies, and Theravada Buddhist temples, Lowell came to include a considerable Cambodian community.

Tontines *in the Cambodian community of Lowell*

Tontines play a critical role in the financial development of Cambodian refugees and are an important source of funding for new businesses and home purchases. The fact that almost every Cambodian in Lowell has a bank account does not stop them from participating in a *tontine*. *Tontines* in Lowell consist of between 15 and 50 members, who each contribute up to $1,000 per month. Unlike many clubs where each member receives the same payout during the cycle, Cambodian *tontines* are examples of 'bidding rotating clubs'. The money collected at each meeting is given to the member who agrees to pay the most in additional payments for the privilege of assuming an earlier position in the rotation. Those who can afford to wait will enjoy payouts greater than their combined contributions, and thus earn a profit on their savings.

Denh, which means 'to bid,' can be tremendously useful to those in need of a large sum. The *tontine* 'master' collects and keeps the money and facilitates the bidding process. The master is responsible for paying on behalf of any member who fails to pay. However, they benefit by being placed in the first position in the rotation of payouts, even before the bidders.

Mrs. Sea, who had been a master of a *tontine* group since she first moved to Lowell in 1982, said '*Tontine* can make you rich and *tontine* can also destroy you'. Mr. Chin, another member, said that the key to a successful *tontine* is trust. Family members fall into the most trustworthy category of membership. The next category includes friends strongly connected through business or worship, and the final trust category consists of colleagues.

Tontines have been transformative for many; members have used their payouts to buy their houses or start small businesses. Mrs. Sous, a long-time member, said, 'my first time playing *tontine* was a success. I opened a Cambodian restaurant'. However, not all participants take advantage of their payout. Mrs. Sous added, 'Most failures are caused by members making poor investments with their payouts. Some Cambodians are addicted to gambling. They get the payout, then gamble at the casino and end up in debt'. Beyond the individual, there is a risk for the *tontine* here, too, if the gambler cannot make their contribution.

Concerns about the trustworthiness of *tontines* has led some to avoid them. Mr. Tim, who works full-time for a famous Angkor dance troupe, moved to Lowell as a refugee in 1982. He and his aunt were active in *tontines* during the 1990s but he is no longer 'playing *tontine*' for fear of being cheated. The fact that a *tontine* has no legal standing increases the risks of the *tontine* master running away with all the money, or a member not making their contribution, given that there is no legal recourse available to those who had been cheated. However, those who take their payout early in a cycle find that the extra amount they pay into the *tontine* is still less than the interest charged by a traditional bank – if they could even qualify. Most 'players' belong to two *tontines*. In this way, they can use the payouts from one *tontine* to contribute to the second.

Ms. Somonita, another long-standing member, is an assistant teacher and the youngest member of a 35-member *tontine* in which she contributes $300 per month. She says that Cambodians born in the US usually do not invest in a *tontine*: 'they don't even know what it is and how it works'. She finds belonging to her *tontine* quite profitable. Though technically her contribution is $300 per month, she actually pays much less. Those who take their payout early pay a substantial premium through their regular contributions. Although her *tontine* has 35 members, only 10 are 'core members,' each with multiple shares. Core members guarantee the contributions of members whom they recruit. In Somonita's case, her contribution is guaranteed by her aunt, a core member of the *tontine*. Not only is this a good risk-mitigation strategy, but it also makes the *tontines* more efficient: masters must collect from core members – 10 members instead of 35.

Since the first settlement of Cambodians in Lowell in the 1970s, *tontines* have allowed new arrivals to help each other build new lives. The younger generation, having seen both the successes and failures of *tontines*, are more reluctant to get involved. The increased accessibility of other financial services such as credit, debit cards, and check-cashing has also contributed to the decline of the *tontine*. Even so, the older generation finds them indispensable.

Uses of *Dhikuti* among Nepali immigrants in Greater Boston

In Boston and the surrounding communities, members of six dhikutis, *the Nepali name for rotating clubs, describe how they operate and use their payouts. The author of these stories is Govinda Raut, then a Hubert Humphrey Fellow at Boston University, and an advisee of Jeff. He is currently a banker in Nepal.*

Introduction

Dhikuti, an informal savings practice in Nepal, has a rich history. It is believed that Himalayan traders initially adapted this practice from clubs started by Tibetan businesspeople. They would use their payouts to fund new ventures. Over time, the practice gained popularity among the Thakali community, who reside between the Mustang and Myagdi districts that straddle the Kali Gandaki Gorge. Eventually, *dhikutis* spread across the country as other communities began replicating the practice. The term 'dhikuti' or 'dhukuti' refers to a treasury box or safe for money, jewellery, and other valuable ornaments (Bajracharya, 2011).

The *dhikutis* operate in the same way as other clubs described in this book: individuals contribute equal amounts to the group pot and take turns withdrawing the payout. In urban areas, particularly among businesspeople, this practice has been modified into a bidding system like those of the Cambodian *tontines*.

Summary of dhikuti *interviews*

During my research, I visited six *dhikutis*. I encountered the first while having lunch at a Nepali restaurant. There, I interviewed Nepali workers who belonged to a *dhikuti*, which led me to a second club, the connections from which led me, in turn, to four more. Club members were willing to discuss their operations, but were hesitant to disclose their names or any information that could identify them. The first visit to a new club was always the most challenging. During subsequent visits members were more comfortable and open. Conversations were purposefully informal and unstructured.

None of the clubs studied practised bidding *dhikutis*. Instead, all members collectively agreed upon the payout order before a cycle began, with negotiation allowed in case of an urgent need.

Club 1: Using technology

The first *dhikuti* I visited included 15 members who each contributed $1,000 per month. The first $15,000 payout went to the organizer. From the second payout onward, each member other than the organizer paid an extra $20 as a thank you for the patience of those who were going to be paid later in the cycle, and the increased risk they took while they awaited their turn. Initially, some members paid cash, but during the pandemic, they switched to Zelle (a US money transfer system owned by major banks). The rule was that if someone failed to pay on time, the organizer took responsibility for ensuring the person expecting their payout received it in full. No late payments were permitted.

Between the first and second cycles, two members relocated and were replaced with two new ones. At the end of the interview the organizer told me he was so occupied with his own business that he was not going to continue leading the club. Unless a new leader steps up, the *dhikuti* will terminate after completing this cycle.

Club 2: Payouts to the homeland

Formed in early 2022, this club consists of 14 male and female members. They hold monthly meetings on the 7th of each month. If any member cannot attend they must inform the group and transfer their contribution to the person receiving the payout for that month. Club members know each other well and share strong social bonds – a point of pride for members. The organizer manages the group without pay, and all members share liabilities and respon-sibilities equally. When I interviewed members, they were about to complete their first cycle and are discussing the possibility of continuing for another cycle.

The payouts are used for sending remittances to Nepal, purchasing a new car, and paying tuition fees. One member used their $14,000 payout to repay a loan, while the remaining funds were used as a down payment on land purchased in Nepal.

Club 3: From weekly pay checks to monthly contributions

This club was formed by a group of women working together at a café. They decided to start their own *dhikuti* to save money for household expenses and emergencies. One of the women, who had been working at the café for more than five years, took charge and initiated monthly savings of $1,000. When asked why they didn't save weekly – their pay checks were weekly – they explained that saving smaller amounts each week would be challenging, especially if someone missed a week of work. Also, the café staff receive $15–20 in daily tips, which account for half of their monthly contributions. They wanted to let their tips accumulate so they could make a sizeable contribution. One member said she plans for her payout to be put towards the purchase of a new car, which would make commuting to work easier and potentially help her find a better-paying job.

Club 4: Building assets in the US; taking care of friends from afar

This club had been active longer than the others I had encountered. The organizer, who immigrated to the US with a visa in 2003, initially encouraged young individuals to come together to save $50 or $100 per month for their collective welfare, but there was not much interest. In 2009, when most had become more settled in Boston with stable jobs, a friend needed money urgently in Nepal. This led to the formation of a *dhikuti* group with 15 or 16 young members so that one payout could go to the friend in Nepal. After completing the first cycle, the organizer stepped down, and the member I met has since become the group's leader.

Initially, the club started with a $500 contribution per member. With each cycle, the club increased the amount: $750, $1,000, $1,250, and $1,500. Nearly 80 per cent of the original members have remained with the rotating club. They used payouts for home renovations and to purchase new houses by combining the payouts from two cycles. Now, almost all members of the *dhikuti* own houses and cars and have stable incomes. When I last met them, they were considering increasing the monthly savings amount to $2,000, but no decision has been made.

Club 5: Business owners investing payouts in the US and abroad

This club collects the highest contributions – $2,000 a month. All 16 members are business owners, hold jobs, or are individuals with strong financial backing. The $32,000 payouts were typically used for their businesses or home renovations. Almost all own their own homes. Sending money to Nepal was common, but members focused on building their own assets in the US.

Club 6: Club funds towards expanding a remittance service

This club includes members with a wider range of incomes. The organizer plays a critical role in fostering trust among members. The organizer only selects individuals who are well known or recommended by existing members. As with many clubs, a new entrant receives their payout in the later months of the cycle. This provision allows the organizer and other members to develop trust in the new member.

During interviews, I had the opportunity to meet a store owner who used his payouts to invest in inventory, make repairs, and purchase store-related items. Additionally, he also ran a remittance agency. Through the *dhikuti*, he was able to network with other Nepali individuals to expand his remittance businesses.

Findings

Productive use: Nearly all *dhikuti* members were using payouts for productive purposes or to accumulate assets. In 2010, for instance, one member purchased a house in Somerville, Massachusetts for $350,000 before selling it in 2022 for $800,000. The family used the proceeds to purchase a new house in Everett for $600,000. In this case, the member gained $200,000 from their initial investment. In such instances, *dhikuti* funds have directly generated significant gains beyond the initial payout.

Agency and creativity: The *dhikuti* members demonstrated their creativity in managing their clubs and handling money. The structured arrangement of *dhikuti* turns, which allowed members to access a significant amount of money within a short timeframe, boosted their confidence and willingness to test new ideas. Additionally, members shared various tips on inventory management, cash flow management, and risk–reward management. Members also found creative solutions to send money to Nepal, despite the document requirements and threshold amounts imposed by regulators.

Business-minded members have effectively managed *dhikuti* payouts to support their enterprises. For instance, a convenience store owner participated in three *dhikutis*. He used the first *dhikuti* to purchase the store, joined the second *dhikuti* after six months and took out the payout after three months to increase his stock. He joined the third *dhikuti* after four months and is continuing to use payouts to grow his inventory.

Prosperity: The use of *dhikuti* payouts has improved the financial situation of almost all members. They have been able to access a substantial amount of money and invest it for immediate or future gain, which may not have been possible through the formal financial systems. While members do not claim that all their prosperity was owed solely to *dhikuti* investments, they agree that the clubs played a major role in their success. The availability of easily accessible funds has given them the confidence to bring their ideas to fruition. One long-time chef, for instance, finally realized his dream of opening a restaurant thanks to his *dhikuti*'s $15,000 payout.

Accountability: In one exceptional case, a *dhikuti* member was unable to meet the club's contribution deadline; he had lost his money gambling. He had struggled to manage his finances and had consistently delayed his *dhikuti* contributions. Other club members worked to help him overcome his gambling addiction and focus on his business. Once someone becomes a *dhikuti* member, he or she is motivated to earn money to make their contributions. Fulfilling financial obligations through a rotating club encourages productivity and minimizes wasteful spending. The hard work and dedication put into meeting commitments serve as a foundation for a better future, promoting economic investment and financial discipline. One *dhikuti* member works from 9.30 a.m. to 9.30 p.m. six days a week to meet household expenses and another works for 60–70 hours a week to meet his *dhikuti* contributions.

Conclusion

Forgoing documentation and bureaucratic procedures, the *dhikuti* practice stands out as an exceptional avenue for accessing finance to invest, manage expenses, and save. Capacity building can play a vital role in further fortifying *dhikutis*. Implementing mobile application-based ledger maintenance, for instance, would streamline and enhance transparency in the accounting process. The success of such initiatives, however, would likely depend on the character and composition of each *dhikuti*, and whether these shifts would be driven by members and organizers or by external actors.

Planning for prosperity: Enduring *dhikutis* in Queens' Nepali communities

Parbati and Ashok, both from the same region in Nepal, met in Queens, New York. Together, they opened a dhikuti *(a rotating club) and, with others, began generating large sums for business ventures and infrastructure investment back home. This story was written by Krishnan Subedi, Jeff's former student.*

With its diaspora concentrated in Queens, Nepali immigrants in New York have levied the strength of *dhikutis*, introduced in the previous case, to realize their vision of the American Dream and improve lives back home. Respondents reported that their communities were concentrated in the neighbourhoods of Elmhurst/Corona, Jackson Heights, and Sunnyside/Woodside. They typically join *dhikutis* to launch businesses to pay for their children's medical expenses and education.

Unlike money clubs in other immigrant communities that complete a cycle within a few months or a year, *dhikuti* cycles run for two to four years or even longer so members can amass sufficient capital to achieve their long-term goals.

During the study, I visited immigrants at home, in shops and restaurants, and during religious activities, social functions, and festivals. I carried out 20 interviews of club members, six in-depth key informant interviews, and participated in a *dhikuti* meeting.

Club members meet monthly and most contribute $1,000 per month, plus another $10 to $20 for a dinner following the monthly meeting. Groups range in size from 30 to 90 members. Unlike many money clubs, these *dhikuti* are bidding clubs. Members who receive their payouts early pay an additional $2,000 to $8,000 during the cycle for the privilege of taking the first positions in the rotation. As in the other bidding clubs, those who receive payouts later receive substantially more than the sum of their contributions – an 'interest payment' in return for their patience.

When asked why being part of a *dhikuti* was necessary, all respondents gave similar answers: starting a small store or investing in a business, building a reserve for emergencies or to save for education and healthcare, sending money to relatives back home, or for religious obligations, such as weddings and funerals.

Trust is the most important criterion for selecting club members. Virtually all are from the same caste, religion, ethnic background, or region of Nepal. Some may have even come from the same village or family.

Although many Nepali immigrants who participate in *dhikutis* are established and own businesses, Nepali *dhikutis* in Queens are unique in how they incorporate new, often undocumented immigrants. The immigrant's family or friends sponsor him or her and make the first two contributions on their behalf. This gives the new member time to find a job. They may work as a dishwasher at a Nepali eatery where they can earn perhaps $2,500 to $3,000 a month, working 10 to 12 hours a day seven days a week. The new member receives their payout immediately, which is used to repay their families in Nepal for the costs of travelling to the US and to pay smugglers along the way. After the first two payouts in the cycle, the new member begins contributing to the *dhikuti*. They then pay in $1,000 a month and an additional $30 or $40 per month in extra payments until the cycle is completed.

Managing a *dhikuti* is complex. The organizer needs to track deposits, total savings, extra payments, and contributions to the social fund for each member. The monthly meetings serve as an opportunity to discuss when and where the club will meet, review the club's by-laws, resolve disputes, and fine late contributors. Given the responsibilities of their roles, organizers are paid for their work by the club.

Parbati and Ashok

When Parbati came to the United States eight years ago, she worked 12 to 14 hours a day contending with a meagre $300 weekly salary and exploitative employers. She moved to New York City in 2012 and found a part-time job as a babysitter in Manhattan. From there she started to create a network of Nepali friends.

One evening, when she went to a restaurant for dinner, she saw many Nepali immigrants eating together for a *dhikuti* party. She asked to join the club but was rebuffed; new members cannot join mid-cycle, they said. With her friend Ashok (from the same region of Nepal) Parbati decided to start her own *dhikuti*. Ashok is well-educated, having completed undergraduate studies in business management. Parbati and Ashok recruited 22 members into their new *dhikuti*. In the beginning, they collected $300 per member, but unfortunately, one member took the payout and disappeared. Parbati and Ashok had to make up the difference. With this experience in mind, they adjusted the club's rules: if a member wanted to invite a new member into the club, the applicant needed three guarantors willing to make good on their contributions, should they default.

In 2015, Parbati and Ashok opened another *dhikuti* with the three-guarantors rule. At the time of my interviews, the club included 40 members and the amount collected increased from $300 to $1,000 per month, generating a $40,000 monthly payout, reflecting their new rule that payouts should only be used for business purposes. Those late to club meetings were fined $5, while missing a meeting incurred a $20 fine.

In February 2016, Parbati and Ashok started yet another club that, as of this writing, includes 91 members. Ashok managed both clubs, receiving a $2,200 combined monthly salary for his efforts.

His responsibilities were significant, as each month he oversaw $40,000 from the older club and $91,000 from the newer one. He mentioned that the newer one would run for another seven to eight years given the large membership. I asked Parbati and Ashok why their clubs were so successful. They said it boiled down to trust-building, training in financial literacy and enterprise, people's knowledge and positive attitudes, savings behaviour, evaluating how borrowers used their payouts, and collectively facing risks and challenges.

The impacts of these clubs extend to Nepal, too; Parbati and Ashok had recently sent $20,000 to their village in Nepal to buy an ambulance. At the same time, they were planning to help build their district's school and roads. As we will see in the next case, some rotating clubs operate within the structures of broader community organizations, which often use club dues or donations to fund similar aid and development projects back home.

A typology of New York *dhikutis*: Joy, support, and remittances in savings and insurance clubs

The author investigates four types of dhikutis *that she uncovered in New York. They include traditional rotating clubs as well as insurance associations. With the support of* dhikutis, *Nepalis have been able to consolidate social ties and launch an array of new businesses. This story was written by Tsechu Doma, a former student of Jeff's.*

Development practitioners scramble to come up with ways to alleviate poverty. Billions of dollars are spent on ideas that seem to work well the first few years, but then fail. But what if the answers were already in place?

Given that nearly half of the borough's residents are foreign-born, it is perhaps unsurprising that we stay in Queens for this case (U.S. Census Bureau, 2010).[1] According to the census, New York City has the largest concentration of Nepali people in the US (U.S. Census Bureau, 2010).[2] Most arrive in the country as low-skilled labourers, and find themselves living close to others from Nepal. As a Nepali-speaking ethnic Tibetan who has spent nearly half my life in Nepal, and lived in Queens for years, I was particularly eager to learn more about the variety of *dhikuti* practices.

The Nepali community in New York witnessed a significant surge in *dhikutis* during the 2000s. Members used the term *'khela'* when describing their meetings, the structures of which are similar to the Bangladeshi case. Unique to these clubs, however, is the maintenance of a $1,000 contribution per person as standard practice.

While conducting research, I was able to identify four types of *dhikutis* and interviewed members of each. The four types are presented in Table 2.

Table 2   Four kinds of *dhikutis*

	Category 1	*Category 2*	*Category 3*	*Category 4*
Type of club	Most common and traditional type of *dhikuti*.	Young, up-and-coming membership. This category is small but rapidly growing.	Women's *dhikutis* where women hail from the same Nepali villages. This is an insurance *dhikuti*, not a rotating one.	An established community group with a savings component. This category is common.
Number of members	21	25	60+	250 families
Gender breakdown of members	14 men, 7 women	11 men, 14 women	Intentionally, all women	Even male and female distribution
Average age of members	45	26	35	32
Average income of members	Less than $30,000 a year	Less than $30,000 a year	Less than $30,000 a year	Less than $30,000 a year
Membership connection	Related to each other or family friends of 20–30 years.	Mostly friends with family connections, some relatives.	All from the same village in Nepal.	All from the same village in Nepal.
Monthly member contribution	$1,000	$,1000	$5 (collects $60 per member per year)	$8.33 (collects $100 per year)
Average years of members' education	7+	12+	10+	9+

(Continued)

Table 2 Continued

	Category 1	*Category 2*	*Category 3*	*Category 4*
Motivation for saving	Providing for family – buying a first home, buying a first car, starting a new business.	Saving to send remittances to Nepal, tuition payment, paying off a debt, and paying for family emergencies.	Social fund created to help village families in need.	Social fund for member families in need.
Activity period of the group	Since early 2013	Since 2014	Since 2007	Since 2005
Members' average years spent in the US	10	7	8	10
Club accounting	The organizer of the group keeps books.	The organizers of the group keep books.	A designated person manages the books.	Democratically elected committee with 2-year terms.
Club accountability	Two in-club guarantors per participant. The organizer is the guarantor for everyone.	Two in-club guarantors per participant. The organizers are the guarantors for everyone.	Unspoken social pressure, no formal rules about payment.	Unspoken social pressure, no formal rules about payment.
Determining turns	Highest bidder in terms of interest rates	Highest bidder in terms of interest rates	N/A	N/A
Where are the funds kept?	Turn member's discretion	Turn member's discretion	Individual's bank account	501 (c) 3 non-profit organization's bank account
Member's view on the club's risk	Very secure and tight-knit club Small chance of runaways	Secure and tight-knit club Small chance of runaways	Possible, but little chance of member negligence	Possible, but little chance of member negligence

One common benefit identified across the club types was their fortification of social connections. 'It's like being back in Nepal', one member said. They also appreciated the discipline and accountability the club offered. Many mentioned that playing *dhukuti* helped them finance their start-up businesses or first homes. One said, 'working long hours cannot make "the American Dream" a reality. Hard work must be combined with investments in children's education, real estate, or businesses'.

However, members worried that the $1,000 monthly contribution excluded new arrivals. Money storage was also a worry; members feared the IRS would track them down if they deposited their contributions into a bank account. Finally, because no legal contracts are in play, they knew they had little recourse if someone were to steal club funds.

Below, I highlight key aspects of each club type.

Club 1: Traditional dhikuti

The majority of this club's 21 members are men between the ages of 40 and 55. Since its inception in the late 2000s, members have amassed considerable social capital and are well-established financially.

Every member was related to at least one other member. All members had arrived in the US in the early 2000s. They started participating in *dhikutis* to prepare for bringing their family members from Nepal to the US, with most families reuniting within three to five years.

Those who had their turns in the first six months of the cycle made investments like buying their first home. Members in the latter turns of the rotation put their payouts towards their children's college funds and to grow their businesses. The order of the payments was determined by the extra amount they paid to the club, such as adding an extra $5 to their $1,000 contribution.

As noted in the table, each person is assigned as a guarantor for two other members, with the organizer serving as the backup guarantor for all members. Although many members had heard horror stories of members in other clubs running away with a payout, none could recall a specific instance in New York when pressed for an example.

Club 2: Up-and-coming young people

Dhikutis like this one, made up of young Nepalis living alone in New York, are growing rapidly. They feel the pressure of sending money home to their Nepali families. Most members are young women in their late 20s and early 30s, sent to the US to earn money for the family. Young women tend to work as babysitters for private families and as housekeepers for hotels.

Close family friends and relatives tie the club together. Many grew up together in Nepal. Like Club 1, this *dhikuti* requires each member to be a guarantor of two other members, and the bidding system operates the same way.

I saw gendered differences in how participants invested their payouts; women mostly use theirs to study to become a nurse, a teacher, or to start day care centres, while the young men want to purchase taxi leases or food carts. Since most are not yet permanent residents or US citizens, they must use cash to start their businesses.

Club 3: Women's Social Savings Group

Informal women's groups in cities like Kathmandu and New York have adapted the *dhikuti* to support families with urgent financial need back home in Nepal. Those living in the Himalayan foothills are particularly vulnerable given the popularity and danger of working as mountaineering guides – many men die, leaving families with nothing.

The New York-based Women from Upper Mustang (a remote region in north-western Nepal) organized the Women's Social Savings Group. Every month members contribute $5 to the bookkeeper. Currently, the account holds more than $50,000.

There are no formal rules on how contributions should be made; in this case, contributions are more like club dues rather than rotating club contributions, nor are there formal repercussions for late or missed payments. Any woman from the same village, regardless of her age or status, can join this group. Many give a year's fee in advance, instead of depositing $5 monthly.

This particular *dhikuti* does not convene every month for festivities. Instead, members unite during their traditional New Year to commemorate the occasion. When I inquired about their perspective on contributing to this fund, one member articulated, 'This serves as our life insurance, health insurance, unemployment compensation, pension – basically everything'. Members are mostly employed as domestic help or salon workers, receiving cash payments off the record. These positions lack formal contracts or legal recognition, compelling these women to establish their own safety net.

The women expressed a heightened sense of community within this group, emphasizing that they enjoyed a more influential voice than in other, male-led *dhikutis*. The shared familiarity among members, either personally or through mutual connections back in Nepal, contributed to the camaraderie. They also found the monthly contribution of $5 affordable. This tight-knit network serves as a valuable resource, facilitating job searches and access to training classes. Moreover, it fosters an exchange of information regarding their children's education and extracurricular activities among the members.

Club 4: The Kyidug, *for happy and suffering times*

A similar, but more social-oriented club, is the *kyidug* (literally translated as 'for happy and suffering times'). The *kyidug* has a rich history rooted in the Mustang district of Nepal and populated by Tibetan Nepalis.

According to the members I interviewed, all Nepali-speaking *kyidugs* have a savings component. Members contribute $50–100 every year. Most *kyidugs* are registered as non-profits in the US. They place the collected dues in the *kyidug*'s bank account. During the traditional New Year, all members of the *kyidug* gather for a gala with an open bar paid for by the club. The celebration is always well organized, and many look forward to it; all *kyidug* members attend the party. Halfway through the event, the *kyidug* collects a certain amount from each family, simultaneously recording each family member in their registry.

A democratically elected committee of seven to ten members governs the *kyidug*, with each member serving a year-long term. The committee determines which family is going through 'happy or sad' times, and decides how to help. When a member is hospitalized, for example, the governing committee pays a visit and gives money to help with expenses. When a member passes away, the *kyidug* provides funeral preparations and financial support. The *kyidug* also makes no-interest loans to families in need. Between 25 and 50 per cent of the *kyidug*'s fund goes towards supporting education and cultural programmes. Recently, there have been some talks on investing *kyidug*'s reserves in social enterprises that will generate revenue.

Currently, one *kyidug* in New York manages a community house, while others are pooling their savings in order to buy one. The vision for the community house is to provide a space for member advancement through training classes and cultural preservation programming.

Conclusion

As seen in multiple cases, *dhikutis* are integral to Nepali social fabric in the US. Seen by members as crucial to pursuing the American Dream, *dhikutis* catalyse personal and collective growth.

The expansion of *dhikutis* in New York City – as in Nepal – has occurred without any external assistance or donor support. Members have taken the initiative in devising their own solutions. Having weathered decades of economic instability in Nepal, community members are accustomed to employing inventive methods for thriving outside of formal financial systems. Even in the financial capital of the world, New York, where the Nepali-speaking community has established a significant presence, *dhikuti* practices continue to play a pivotal role – everyone knows at least two or three people participating in a *dhikuti*.

This grassroots approach has yielded impressive impact, fostering the growth of a diverse array of businesses within the community. Nepali-run enterprises, including travel agencies, day care centres, churches, temples, restaurants, food carts, tax firms, law offices, taxi companies, newspapers, remittance centres, grocery stores, import/export shipment companies, printing firms, design agencies, clothing stores, and fast-food processors, have flourished. The success of many of these ventures can be directly attributed to the enabling force of *dhikutis*.

Notes

1. U.S. Census Bureau (2010) 'Quick Facts: Queens County, New York' [website], U.S. Census Bureau. https://www.census.gov/quickfacts/fact/table/queenscountynewyork/PST045222
2. U.S. Census Bureau (2010) 'Quick Facts: Queens County, New York' [website], U.S. Census Bureau. https://www.census.gov/quickfacts/fact/table/queenscountynewyork/PST045222

CHAPTER 3

Case studies of clubs with African roots

Lessons on building community in a Burundian *ikirimba*

Along with credit cards and personal bank loans, a Burundian migrant in Maine also uses an ikirimba *rotating club as a financial tool. Although difficult to get off the ground, funds from this system are still useful in saving and sending money home. The author of this case is Ella Duncan, Kim's former student. The story of her respondent is written in the first person.*

I arrived in Portland in May of 2017 with my wife and two oldest children – my youngest son was born here. We came because I won the American visa lottery. When I was still in Burundi, it was recommended that I come to Portland because of its many Burundians. It helps to start with people you know. I was in good hands with the Burundian community, who helped me while I was waiting to start working.

Back in Burundi, I worked for 10 years with an NGO as their finance manager and as a programme manager. I was part of managing a project on self-help community savings groups, providing training on financial record-keeping. We had a project to help the HIV-positive population run *ikirimbas* [Burundian rotating clubs].

In that same workplace, my colleagues in a group home and I had an *ikirimba* – I was even the president! We were called the 'Best Friends Group'. There were 12 members, including my wife and me. The *ikirimba* was considered a benefit of my job and the regular contribution was made directly from our salaries. We would each put in 100,000 BIF [approximately US$75], rotating the payout each month.

Using this *ikirimba*, my wife and I were able to compile enough savings so that when we made the journey to America, we didn't need to borrow from anyone. But the journey was expensive;

it depleted all our savings. When we arrived, I only had $300 in my pocket.

When we were first getting settled in Portland, I joined an *ikirimba*. I had started working in a group home (an extended care facility for elderly, disabled, or medically challenged people), and my colleagues had asked me to join their *ikirimba*. I contributed $200 to this club each month. I used the payouts to help repay personal loans and to prepare for the winter; I bought warm clothes for my family and prepared for housing and car costs in the cold months. This club has strict rules and penalties; you need to pay on time. Members are colleagues from work, so everyone knows we all get paid on Friday. You need to contribute by Saturday; otherwise, interest and fines begin on Sunday.

Starting an *ikirimba* is difficult. Everything is communicated on a WhatsApp group. Everyone understands the concept – that's easy – but people might not be sufficiently comfortable with the rest of the members to disclose personal information. Finding the right amount to contribute is also tricky. Some may find the contribution too high to be affordable, while others find it too low to be worthwhile. So, you work on the relationships first. One approach is to build affinity, in the same way I joined colleagues in the group home.

Among us Burundians, we have other approaches to community savings. We have a general collection of money in our community into an association, which behaves less like an *ikirimba* and more like a funeral insurance system. For example, last week, someone here in the US lost his brother. He needed money to bring the body back home. He messaged the Burundian WhatsApp group and asked for contributions, and we collected $4,000 to assist him. Inspired by this, some colleagues and I are thinking about creating a funeral fund, with monthly contributions that are only distributed when needed. It's not the same as an *ikirimba*, but it's also useful. The Burundian community in Canada already started such a fund. It works like this: a small amount is given by many, many people, and there are levels of support available for funerals according to the relationship with the lost person. So, you receive different amounts for losing your mother versus losing your cousin.

This kind of fund is useful because we Africans have a lot of family back home who all expect those who have immigrated to the US to send money home. Even I used to think that if someone would send only $100 home, they must be selfish! But now I know how hard it is. I experience all the expenses immigrants must struggle with here in the US, yet my family and friends in Africa don't understand. They only see what we can have, not how hard it is to get it and to keep it.

Things are difficult right now because my wife is not working. She was in an internship programme recently, but that is ending. She could only work three days a week for 24 hours. She can't work more than that because day care is too expensive, so someone needs to stay home with our children. This is a problem for many families. Day care is too expensive, but without it, you can't work.

At the moment, I am not in any rotating club. I am focusing on starting a business. Together with my colleagues, we want to open our own group home. I manage my finances through credit, savings, and personal loans from banks. After using my salary to pay down loans and credit cards, I save the rest for my business. I am also using my tax returns to invest in the business.

Reflections on struggle, community, and savings in Portland, Maine

Friendship blossomed within a Burundian ikirimba *in Portland, Maine, creating a sense of security. This informant explains the push factor for joining a rotating club, and the motivation to start their version to support a growing wedding planning business. This story was documented by Ella Duncan, Kim's former student. She is writing it from the perspective of the* ikirimba *member.*

I've been in Portland since 2014. My first idea was to go to a big city and live there. I first arrived in Maryland, close to Washington, DC, and saw how people were rushing – it was too much! But I was impressed by how people were living, by how different it was, and by how differently people acted – even men were cooking! I didn't know what to do, but I had friends here in Portland who told me, 'come here, there is a community of Burundians, join us.' My sister was in Portland before me, and my mom has come after my second daughter was born.

When I first arrived, my sister was staying in the shelter overflow at a local motel with her kids. Coming from Burundi on the equator, that first winter was very hard. We didn't have guidance. We didn't even know how to ride the bus! We had to figure everything out ourselves. We would visit the General Assistance office, but you can go every day for a week from 6 a.m. to 2 p.m. and still not receive a voucher to go grocery shopping.

I was lucky that I could stay with a friend and didn't have to stay in a city shelter. She already had a work permit and had been able to get an apartment. At that time, when I had first arrived, the state's General Assistance was helping me with rent and food.

I would cook for one friend's family because they weren't allowed to cook in their shelter. Her son went to school close to me, so I would send the meals home with him. My sister would come to stay with me during the day because she wasn't allowed to be in the motel during the daytime. To fill the days, my sister and I would spend time on the bus, buying tickets and just riding it wherever it was going around the city; the America I saw on the TV was not the one I was living in.

I often thought about going back to Burundi, but attending a local church changed my mind. I made friends, and I saw other people going through what I was going through. Church members gave me advice. While I waited to start working, I volunteered to try and get American work experience to match what I had studied in school. When I started working as a direct support health professional, I started to feel that things could change. I worked until the birth of my youngest daughter, one year ago, and I hope to go back to school to become a social worker.

I had heard there were rotating clubs among Burundians in Portland. I couldn't join at first because I didn't have cash. To be a part of a club, every two weeks I had to contribute $200. I had bought a car and was struggling to save for car loan payments against all other expenses, like sending money back home and paying rent. The *ikirimba* gave me the help I needed to start saving.

Here in Portland was my first time in such a club, I didn't participate in Burundi. I learned about it from a colleague who said it was helpful to her because she had a big family, and it gave her space for her own expenses. Then I joined with my sister, and she brought her friends. It was social. We could also meet and talk about other things.

For me with the *ikirimba*, the benefit was that you get to make more friends. I need money out of the *ikirimba*, sure, but the social engagement is very important as well. If you come here and you are married with kids, you won't meet anyone. You don't have any of your own money. You are depressed. But in an *ikirimba*, everyone can speak honestly about their struggles because you are in something together. I believe it's typical for many people in Portland to be in *ikirimbas*, but it is not something people talk about openly. You only talk about it with people you are close to. Finances are private.

Ikirimbas require trust, and so you get close with those people you save with. You see them in other activities. They become like close family, always there for you. When my first daughter was born, my *ikirimba* group threw me three baby showers. That wasn't about saving; that was just about supporting friends.

I stayed in the *ikirimba* until my daughter was born. When I stopped working, it became too much to keep contributing to the *ikirimba* because you can't miss a payment. Although joining requires making a commitment to stay, I explained to them that I couldn't keep contributing. As I have explained, it was a group of my close friends, and so they were more lenient. Someday, when I can save again, they will let me back into the club.

I am also starting my own *ikirimba*. Jean's wife, myself, and three other friends started a small company, and we also save together. We wanted to be more proactive in our lives and finances, and we saw we had skills useful for planning weddings. To start, we saved small amounts together, which we used to purchase *mvutanus* [traditional Burundian dress] and other things you need for a traditional Burundian wedding. Once we had those products, we began to rent them out and found there was demand even out of state! During this most recent wedding season, we did four weddings for Rwandans, Burundians, and Congolese. We are hoping that next year will be even bigger.

Our approach to saving for the wedding business was different from our approach to other rotating clubs. Only two of us were working at the time – our primary goal was to create an opportunity for us to work. With that goal as the focus, there wasn't a strict requirement of amounts for everyone to put in at one time. Instead, we set goals with three-month timelines. For example, if we knew we needed $1,000 to buy fabrics, we would make a timeline in which everyone could contribute their portion at any point during those three months. Throughout the three-month window, we would have meetings and remind each other of the commitment, but if necessary, we would also lend internally without interest. We knew it was tough, but we needed that commitment from everyone.

Customers have asked us to manage the decorations for their whole wedding. So, we plan to take the money we've made so far and invest in buying everything we need to run an event.

Women-led savings in Somali *ayuutos*

The United States was full of surprises for this Somali migrant, challenging their idea of the American Dream. To meet their needs in Massachusetts, this migrant joined a traditional Somali ayuuto, *rotating clubs predominantly run by and for women, based in Texas. Lessons in* ayuutos *include the need to network with older Somali women, viewed as more reliable in this cultural rotating club. Jayshree Venkatasan is the author of this story, writing from the perspective of her informant. She is Kim's former student.*

I came to the US in 1999 when I was nine years old. My family had come to Kenya to escape the [Somali] Civil War in 1991 when I was a one-year-old. My parents, brother, sister, and I lived together until my father moved to the US when I was seven years old. Since he sent money back home, we didn't have to struggle with finances as other families did. I don't remember why my father moved to the US, but he was working here doing odd jobs and then found work as a parking attendant. But he is great with handling money, so he managed to send us money and build our savings before petitioning for us to join him in the US.

My parents – particularly my mother – have always been a part of Somali rotating clubs, called *ayuutos*. My mother lives in Texas, and she is a member of many different *ayuutos*. Each one is used for a different reason. For example, she uses some clubs to get money to restock her store, which she purchased in 2008 after selling a Shell gas station she ran. Other *ayuutos* are used for other goals. My mother has a good reputation in the Somali community in Texas, and it's because of her that I got involved in my first *ayuuto* two years ago.

My father and I decided to take a position in an *ayuuto* in Texas that my mother was a part of. We had huge credit card debt and my mother suggested that we should use the *ayuuto* to repay it. So, we joined a group with 10 members who each contributed $1,000 every month. We call each contribution a 'leg', so this *ayuuto* had 10 legs. Some men join *ayuutos*, but it's mostly women. Also, it's mostly older women, not our generation. Before the *ayuuto* starts, the women meet to discuss everyone's needs in order to determine their position in the queue to receive the lump sum payout. We were content with a later spot in the cycle because we were only joining to save rather than to borrow, as members earlier in the cycle were doing. My mother was also part of the same *ayuuto*, but she wanted a spot early in that group. The group also decides the day on which the money is to be contributed every month. Everyone knows the order in which the payout takes place, and everyone keeps their own records. On the day that the contribution is decided, people withdraw the cash and give it to the person whose turn it is to receive the money.

Because my father and I were in Boston and my mother was in Texas, I would transfer my mother $1,000, which she would withdraw from her account to give to whoever was receiving the payout. The payout is always in cash because if the person suddenly gets $10,000 in their bank account, they'll have to explain it. Since my father and I lived in a different state, our payment was sent, like our monthly contribution, by bank transfer. We used the payout to pay off credit card debt.

I liked the result of having $10,000. It's always hard to save like this alone. Being in a club provides discipline, motivation, and a sense of community ... banks don't have a service like this for small business owners. But there was also the stress of making sure we had the money by the decided date every month – we had to tighten our belts to ensure that we had enough money to send.

I would definitely join an *ayuuto* again, but I need to find a club of older women who will accept me. I don't want to do this with someone my age. My sister and her friends once had an *ayuuto* for $2,000, which was much smaller, but it led to huge fights. People would not respect the contribution date and things got lax. However, if there is an older person in the group, there is some authority, and participants won't be sloppy; you must be respectful of the *ayuuto*.

My father used to run a store with some friends, but he bought them out two years ago. It became a fully owned family business, which I still help my father run. My dream is to make this the best store in this neighbourhood. There are no other stores nearby where you can even get a coffee. I want to have a café, a deli – but it's not easy! I am now in the middle of paperwork with the Boston Health Commission. I also want to make sure I know what to stock and how to stock it. There are many challenges, but I am hopeful that this can be a success.

Upato help Tanzanians plan while living in a new place

For Tanzanians, an upato *offers support for funeral insurance or other major life events. Rukia explains how she tried several different savings groups in Massachusetts until she found the right fit. In Rukia's words,* upato *is an essential lifeline not only in the US but also back home in Tanzania. This story was written by Bamzi Banchiri Omaita, Kim's former student.*

'Saving is challenging. We have two lives – you live here and then you live the same life back at home. Everything that's there, you're living it too. One of the things that's really helpful is *upato*.'

Rukia seeks to balance these two lives – and their respective obligations – alongside her husband and child in Massachusetts. She has been involved in multiple savings groups, which have been critical in her financial journey. She recently purchased a plot of land in Dar-es-Salaam using money that she accumulated in one of her *upatos*. The following are her words:

I started doing it with smaller groups immediately after I arrived in 1999. After being swindled in my first two groups, I joined two clubs from other communities; a Congolese club and Kenyan club. These groups worked really well and this time I didn't lose money.

Then, I joined an *upato* with seven other Tanzanian members. The money would sit in a bank account before we divvied up the pot. The goal was for every member to receive $10,000. We divided club members into two groups: the four members who received the payout money of $10,000 after the first four months and the four members who received $10,000 during the next four months. After both groups had received their payout, I decided not to go back because I did not have the financial capacity to continue contributing for that lengthy duration. I decided to join another club, in which each member would contribute about $180 per week, to receive $540 each month. This ended in November. We were supposed to start another cycle in December, but some members pulled out and it ended.

The $10,000 that I had received from the eight-member *upato* came at a time when I didn't have a job, so part of it went into paying debts that I had owed, and part of it I used it to buy a plot of land in Dar-salaam since I don't even know if I am going to be here long; the President's announcement has made a lot of us scared. I have been thinking about Tanzania for a while even though I'm not ready to move. I still need to work and save more. But I had to save to buy a plot. That was the first step. I'm planning to build a house just in case anything happens with my situation.

Right now, I'm not doing anything with the plot and I'm just allowing one gentleman to grow cassava on it, but I don't charge him. At least I know that the land is being taken care of, and my son and daughter check it regularly.

I plan to try to start building this year, and the best way of saving is by using an *upato*. Without an *upato*, when anybody cries, I run [away]. Saving in an *upato* means that I have a little left to share [when anybody cries]. I have shared sometimes and struggled with whatever else was left, but I was happy knowing that I had saved. If I want to do anything big, then I will look into an *upato*.

Wakanda with Valentines

Now, I'm in a club with nine other women who share common interests. We support each other whenever there's bereavement, but we thought we could also do it for fun and try to start a business with it. We started contributing $50 every month into a bank account. Not only do we pay the $50, but we must pay it by the 25th of each month, or else you are required to pay $10 as a fine.

We don't have a savings account, but we have a checking account. We figured that the money was just sitting there, so we decided to explore business ventures. We have held two events. One was a Valentine's event in 2019 and then we also did a Wakanda event [based on the fictional home of the superhero Black Panther]. It was good and many people started asking if we would do them again. All events are paid for by participants, who receive dinner and join in African dancing. It was challenging – we didn't break even, especially on the Wakanda event.

With the savings that we had, we came up with an idea and decided to use this money within the club. We started lending money to club members. A member can borrow a maximum of $2,000 at 10 per cent interest.

The money is contributed by each member into a joint bank account. The account is managed by the chairperson and the secretary, but the account information is available to any member. Now with Cash App, they can send their deposit straight to the bank account.

We started with very high spirits, but now we are struggling with the monthly contributions. On the 25th of last month, we set a deadline for all remaining loans to be settled. We wanted to distribute funds back to members. Every member in the group owes some money and we set a deadline so that everyone would clear their balances, but until now we haven't received anything – other expenses are taking priority.

We started investigating real estate as an investment. Currently, we have $10,000 saved, excluding the loan balances owed to the club. If all balances are cleared, we would have more than $20,000.

Funeral insurance upato

We started a funeral money club, an insurance club, in 2006 to help Tanzanian community members cover burial costs. When a member dies, the other members will contribute a certain amount to reach a total of $15,000. But because we already have money in a bank account, the $15,000 can be paid immediately to the member's family. Then the rest of the members would contribute the amount required to replace the $15,000 that has been withdrawn. For example, if we have 1,000 members, each person would contribute $15 to go towards replacing the $15,000. When we first started, we could only pay $4,000 for each death because we didn't have many members. Each one of us at the time contributed $30 for each death that occurred. Currently, we have more than 1,000 members in the United States, and our contribution is thus $15. Our goal is to have 5,000 members and reduce individual contributions to $3 per death.

You become an active member when you put in $110, but you must wait before you can benefit. At the beginning, the waiting period was three months before they could receive or make contributions to any death events. The waiting period has now increased to six months because we had a few cases of members joining when they were very sick and would die a few months later.

You must be in the US to join, but after you are a member you can go anywhere in the world. The $15,000 will follow you as long as you're maintaining your membership by paying $20 at the beginning of the year and contributing to each death. We have had two deaths in Tanzania of members who had moved back home from the US. Both members received the full insurance amount because we could confirm that they were active members. Since 2006, when the group was first started, we have contributed over $110,000 towards burial costs. Members no longer need GoFundMe because of this community. The only way a non-Tanzanian can become a member is if they are married to a Tanzanian person.

The only thing that we are seeing is the increase in burial costs. In the future, we need to look into the fact that $15,000 might not be enough or decide that instead of contributing $3 with 5,000 members we could contribute $6 so that each member's family is receiving much more than $15,000.

Another advantage is that kids under the age of 18 do not have to contribute anything. If a member's child dies while that member is still active, the family receives $15,000 as long as the child is registered when the member first joins the group.

We have a board with the usual positions: a president, chairman, secretary, treasurer, and everything else. Anytime someone passes away, information will be shared with the president. After verifying that the death has happened, the board will meet to see how many people are eligible to contribute and determine the amount that each member needs to contribute. After they meet and discuss, they release the money to the family and let the rest of the members know how much each member is required to contribute to rebuild the fund. When a contributing member joins, they also decide who should benefit after they die. They register the beneficiary or a charity to whom their money should be given.

Funding funerals: Ethiopian cab drivers in Boston

For generations, communities in Ethiopia have managed their financial needs and risks through informal mutual aid associations. The most prominent of these associations include the iddir, *an emergency and funeral insurance group. This case study focuses on the* iddir *practised in Boston, Massachusetts. The author is Elizabeth Mengesha, Kim's former student.*

The iddir

Solomon is the chairman of an *iddir* among Ethiopian taxi drivers, officially called the Ethiopian Taxi Drivers' Funeral Association. Now in his mid-50s, Solomon arrived in Boston in 1985 to continue his studies at a local university. To earn money, Solomon drove a taxi. After his studies, he worked as an engineer for nearly a decade. Tired of his regimented work life, Solomon went back to taxi driving.

In 2008, Solomon and five other drivers discussed the idea of starting an *iddir* after the death of a fellow Ethiopian taxi driver. The decision was provoked by observing the struggles the deceased taxi driver's family endured in paying for funeral expenses. Given the elaborate nature of Ethiopian funerals and the customary practice of returning the deceased to Ethiopia for burial, funeral-related costs can be exorbitant.

Structure and operation

Solomon explained that almost everyone who had been raised in Ethiopia was involved in an *iddir* in some way. In his case, his parents were involved in a neighbourhood *iddir*. He noted that in Ethiopia, joining the neighbourhood *iddir* was expected, and was understood as the community's way of collectively managing the risk of emergencies.

The Ethiopian Taxi Drivers' Funeral Association is a registered non-profit organization that adheres to a formal structure and strict by-laws. The club is explicitly non-political and non-religious. Its main purpose is to fund emergencies related to death, but can also include illness. Membership is exclusive to Ethiopian taxi drivers; a hackney (taxi) licence is required for entry.

The basic requirement for members is a monthly contribution of $30 per member. With approximately 100 people currently in the club, this amounts to an average of $3,000 per month for a total of $36,000 annually. The leadership includes an executive committee of four officers – a chairman, secretary, treasurer, and auditor – and three members who oversee the association's management in conjunction with the officers.

Despite the overall formal structure of the organization, the system for collecting deposits is rather fluid. Members are required to simply give their contribution to members of the executive committee before the end of each month, which normally happens through casual run-ins on the taxi route. Solomon explained that this system works efficiently and removes the need to hold meetings every month. The executive committee maintains regular communication with association members through an email list. Upon handing their money to an executive committee member, members are issued an official receipt of deposit. Collected money is given to the treasurer, who then deposits it in the organization's bank account. The treasurer also keeps track of all transactions through a bookkeeping system, which is overseen by the auditor.

The executive committee meets once a month to discuss club operations and to decide on the use of funds when a crisis emerges. When a decision is made to dedicate funds for an emergency, money can only be withdrawn from the bank with the signatures of the chairman, treasurer, and secretary. According to the by-laws, funds can be used for all matters related to death and serious illness. Benefits extend to members' spouses and children under 18.

In the event of a group member's death, the *iddir* plays a key role in facilitating all tasks related to the *lekso* (mourning customs) and funeral arrangements. Immediately after the death, the executive committee meets to divide the various tasks among group members. These tasks range from coordinating with the funeral home and arranging to have the body sent back, to figuring out who will pick up food and rental chairs for the *lekso*. During the *lekso*, group members take the lead in distributing bread and drinks to attendees. The wives of taxi drivers (most members of the association are men) are expected to assist with preparing food for the *lekso* and funeral lunches. At the funeral services, *iddir* members usually serve as pallbearers.

Benefits of participation

The benefits of participating in the *iddir* are clear. It is an efficient way to insure against emergencies, particularly death-related expenses, involves very little commitment of time and money, and offers low transaction costs. Given that many Ethiopians are accustomed to the concept of mutual aid associations, little explanation is needed to attract new members.

Solomon explained that everyone in the club has at least one bank account, which suggests that members are not isolated from formal financial systems. Rather than serving as a substitute for a formal service, the *iddir* offers help that club members cannot easily find in the formal sector.

Within the club, there are cohorts of members who are close friends. In one example, a taxi driver fell seriously ill two months after joining the group. Although he had been part of the *iddir* for only a short time, Solomon said he was still seen as a member of the association; group members visited him during his hospitalization and offered comfort to the family. Additionally, a core group of his friends continued to pay his contribution to the *iddir* in his absence. A few months later, when the taxi driver died, *iddir* funds were used to pay for his funeral.

Solomon took pride in telling me that *iddir* members were providing 'great community work'. *Iddir* members, should they experience a death, receive not only financial support but also assistance with funeral logistics. The moral support of the *iddir* is a powerful social benefit, given that most Ethiopian immigrant families lack the same type of extended family they once had. Solomon also mentioned that *iddir* members get special recognition by the priest and other community leaders during funeral services. In recognizing the *iddir*'s positive impact on the broader Ethiopian community in Boston, Solomon highlights why so many of the clubs described in this book succeed: they affirm and maintain familiar social and cultural practices for their members. While not all successful clubs involve a strong communal spirit, it is apparent that those that do both further the financial benefit of those involved – via advice and collaboration – and help anchor members socially and culturally in a new place.

Social and money clubs for Eritreans in Seattle

Equob is a traditional, deeply rooted form of rotating club practised in Eritrea. Eritrean immigrants in the Seattle, Washington, area have carried these traditions with them with the hope of passing them on to their children. As a result, the equob is a savings and social-gathering tradition that Eritrean immigrants still practise today. The club has also expanded to include another type of money club: the savings and loan club. The author of this report is Filimon Ghebretinsae, Jeff's former student.

My grandmother said, 'Back in Eritrea, these types of groups are very common among middle-income women and have proven to be very effective'. My grandmother's *equob* in Seattle consists of 10 women – five retired and five who are still working. They all met at church and over time became friends. My grandmother says, 'Since we were close friends and we trusted each other, I proposed that we start an *equob*.' She told me that this is a great way to stay connected outside of church and strengthen their friendship. Her friends agreed that forming an *equob* would give them a chance to spend more time with each other while saving money. During my interview, my grandmother said, 'Back in Eritrea, my *equob* had more than 50 women'. However, here in the United States it is hard to find a group of women that trust each other and have the time to participate in an *equob*. An additional constraint is that members are required to speak Tigrinya so that all members can be understood.

The club of 10 meets monthly and each contributes $100 to the fund. Payments rotate, with each member receiving their payout in turn. Each member also contributes another $20 to build a savings and loan fund. At the end of each meeting, the $1,000 payout is given to the predetermined member, who also acts as host for that meeting. The host prepares food and performs a traditional coffee ceremony, making the event very festive. The $20 additional payment from each woman is deposited into a lockbox. The woman who receives the payout is charged with keeping the lockbox until the next meeting where it is passed to another member. During the subsequent meeting, the money is counted in front of the entire group and the *equob* bookkeeper notes the usual loan fund deposit of $200 per meeting, equating to $2,400 per year. The funds are lent out to members according to the club's by-laws.

My grandmother added, 'Back in Eritrea, we used *equob* payouts to pay for school fees, to buy clothing and livestock, or to start small businesses'. However, here in the US, members use their payouts to send money back to family in Eritrea and to cover personal expenses such as rent.

Traditionally in Eritrea, *equobs* are common among women yet rare among men. However, surprisingly, in Seattle, there are many Eritrean *equobs* for men. The ones I found varied from 10 to 40 members. Like my grandmother's clubs, the purpose of many of these *equobs* is both financial and social. My uncle belongs to a truck drivers' *equob* with 10 members, who each save $500 per month. Besides saving, they have occasional dinners and drinks to stay connected. Some of these men were friends in Eritrea. My uncle says, 'Our initial meetings were so fun and encouraging that we wanted to do more and help one another, and decided to start an *equob*'. His *equob* has been running for about five years.

Soon, the *equob* will shift so that the payout will not go to members but instead to a special fund. After two years, the group will use the fund to invest in businesses such as restaurants, shops, houses, or gas stations.

My uncle says, 'We have not had a case where a member was unable to make his $500 monthly contribution'. Were that to happen, *equob* rules would require them to pay double the next month. They are planning to increase their monthly contributions to $1,000 per member in the next cycle and restrict membership to those who can afford this amount.

My uncle's *equob* was inspired by other immigrant rotating clubs in the Seattle area, of which there are many, including a large Ethiopian *equob*. My uncle says, 'Ethiopians' *equobs* can have as many as 100 members, but in my opinion, that is too many, because it may take years before it is your turn to collect money'. Small groups keep things close and personal. Bigger groups usually have associations and more resources available to them.

Kenyan *chamas* in New Hampshire

Retirement houses in Kenya, funeral costs, and weddings: when it comes to funding these important life events, rotating clubs offer an opportunity to save. The case discusses the utility of Kenyan chamas *and how a communal culture reinforces the* chamas' *success. The author of these stories is Carolyn M. Musyimi-Kamau, a connection of Jeff's.*

Carolyn is a member of two rotating clubs, or *chamas*, made up of women from Kenya who are living in the United States, one with 15 members and the other with 30 members. Her husband is a member of an all-male *chama* with five members.

Carolyn's club

Four years ago, Carolyn organized a *chama* with 15 members from eight states across the country. They meet by phone the third Sunday of every month. The members save $163 each month. Of this amount, $130 goes to their investment fund in Kenya to purchase houses for their retirement, $20 to a vacation fund, $20 for an emergency 'kitty', and $3 for the wire transfer fee. The kitty is used to provide a decent funeral for the members, their parents, and their immediate relatives, or for a wedding. They deposit contributions into M-PESA, the best-known mobile money provider in Africa, and receive 7 per cent per year in their Kenyan shillings account. They are considering another fund that will provide them with an 11 per cent return on their savings. The amount to be paid out for the death of a relative or family member is spelled out in the club's by-laws. With the interest M-PESA paid on their savings, members recently travelled to Jerusalem and the Holy Land (all members are Christians). As with many of the clubs described here, the *chama* has strict written rules and the group sticks to them. For example, meetings start exactly on time and last no more than an hour. If someone contributes late, they must pay double the amount when they do contribute.

Several members work in the healthcare industry, providing compassionate support to elders. They receive $2,800 per month, or $33,600 per year, and are each saving almost $2,000 per year in this *chama* alone. Many in the club are members of other *chamas*.

Carolyn's husband's club

Carolyn's husband's *chama* has five members. Each contributes $200 per week. All members are Kenyans. The money is being used to start a home-care business in Methuen, Massachusetts that members own collectively.

General comments

Carolyn estimates that 80 per cent of local Kenyans here are part of similar *chamas*. 'We are from a social community. We do things together,' she says. Through participation in their *chamas*, Carolyn and her husband have seen a clear change in how members save. Without the club, they would never have saved this much. She believes that most immigrants have bank accounts, but they are better able to save through their *chamas*. Carolyn said she would be very interested in teaching what she learned about savings and rotating clubs to non-immigrants in New Hampshire.

Solidarity and support: Ivorian associations in the US

Remy and his wife Martine are active members of an Ivorian 'association', used primarily as an insurance mechanism, which makes it an insurance club. Membership is based on one's Ivorian identity and emphasizes trust. By saving money collectively, Ivorian migrants in the US can cover funeral expenses for their family members back home in Africa and even splurge on social gatherings from time to time. Charlie Williams is the author of this story. She is a former student of Kim's.

Originally from Côte d'Ivoire, Remy and his wife Martine arrived in the US in 2002. Remy worked at the Ivorian embassy in Washington, DC, while Martine served as a nanny in the area. After Remy's embassy job ended, Martine said the family chose not to return to Côte d'Ivoire out of fear of bringing their children back to a country at war. Eventually, after their four children grew up and graduated from school, the parents made their way to Massachusetts to work.

What is an association?

Since their time in Washington, DC, Remy and Martine have participated in what they call an *association*, a type of money club used among Ivorian immigrant communities for an array of purposes, but most often for covering funeral expenses. Americans might perceive these clubs to be a type of informal 'funeral insurance' system, although Remy says, 'We don't have the notion of insurance ... we don't think of it that way. It's all about solidarity'.

The association is run by a president and executive board, on which Remy currently serves as the secretary. The club is nationwide, although most members are concentrated in Maryland, Washington, DC, and Virginia. Often, associations are grouped by ethnicity. Martine explains that there are 72 different ethnicities in Côte d'Ivoire, and that associations set up by immigrants in the US still fall mostly along those ethnic lines. For example, because Remy is from western Côte d'Ivoire, he is a member of a western Ivorian association.

The mechanics of an association

Martine compares the association to a *tontine*, a broadly West African type of club. However, unlike *tontines* which routinely rotate payouts, Martine and Remy's association follows a different, flexible model based on need and loyalty.

To join the association, members must pay dues, plus $100 upfront for new members. Then, the new member contributes $10 every month for three months to become eligible for a payout. Most members bring their money in cash to the association's regular meetings, which occur at the end of the month. Other members deposit directly into the club's bank account. Remy says all members have access to the account number to make their deposits. Parents are contributing members, but not their children. Even adult children are not contributing members. If a child loses their parents, then they will join the association. All members must be in good standing to receive money in the form of a payout.

After making regular contributions for at least three months, members may receive full benefits from the club. For example, in the case of the death of a parent, a member may receive a payout from the association to cover funeral costs or lost income due to illness. Payouts range from $2,000 to $12,000 and vary depending on the requirements for travel or funeral costs. Most payouts are in cash, but Western Union is used on occasion if the situation is complicated, and the member cannot receive the cash directly.

Payouts to members are tiered by participation and familial relationships. For instance, if a member were to lose a parent and that member always paid their dues on time, then the association would come together to financially support that member in their period of hardship. If a member were to lose a cousin or sister, and that member had paid their dues on time, then the association has no fixed payout amount to that family, but decides on a case-by-case basis, driven largely by the burial's location.

Additionally, if an active member who has suffered a loss has many friends, some members will contribute additional money to the club's fund which increases the amount that person receives. This is an informal way of determining how much money is given to the claimant and is entirely situational, based on the need and the claimant's popularity within the association.

For example, there was a man named Mr. Tape who was an association member for 10 years. When he died, the association paid $12,000 for two of his closest friends to take his body back to Africa for burial, as he had no family in the US. This significant outlay was seen as appropriate since Mr. Tape was a beloved and long-standing association member.

Most of the time members use their payouts to cover funeral expenses in Côte d'Ivoire. However, Martine explains that not all payouts are directed to funeral expenses. The association may also choose to give a gift to a member to say congratulations for an event such as a wedding, birth, or school graduation. A standard wedding gift is between $500 and $1,000 and would be funded by individual member contributions and not from the club's fund.

In some cases, the association may issue loans to members. The largest loan ever given was to Mr. Tape. Martine and Remy insisted that it was very rare, but the group lent him a one-time sum of $1,500 to cover his rent and bills while he was ill. These sums are negotiated on a case-by-case basis. First, a member – in good standing and with at least three months of association participation – must meet with the executive board to ask for help. The board then assesses the person's reliability before deciding on their case and informing the rest of the members. Remy says that the person asking for the loan must prove that they will repay the loan. The terms of the loan are fairly flexible and interest-free. For example, if a member is sick, the association might decide that the loan does not need to be repaid. When Martine's daughter was sick and needed surgery, for instance, she was out of work for a week and the association lent her $500. There is no formal amount of time for repayment in the case of illness. Association leadership determines the amount based on need.

Not all business: Social elements of the association

Martine and Remy smile as they share their association's social perks. Martine remarks that sometimes members offer to host meetings. She laughs and adds, 'But, you have to cook!' The relationships between members remain important even as members leave the club. 'We know each other,' Martine adds, 'we are still friends'.

The club's parties are events worth waiting for. Leadership looks for large venues that can host groups of 2,000 people or more and are open late into the night, as a typical party ends at around 3 a.m. Martine noted that members often show up late as they are on 'African time'. The association pays for the venue, but members are encouraged to bring both family and friends even if they do not belong to the association. Club money pays for an array of party benefits: the venue, decorations, photographer, and DJ cost between $7,000 and $8,000, and are taken from the association's dues. Some clubs pay for catering as well but mostly members bring food in a potluck fashion. The parties are lively and loud with lots of festive attire on display. Every summer, Martine and Remy make the trip from Massachusetts to Maryland, the home of their club, to attend its annual gala.

Looking ahead

The association continues to meet regularly and serves as a useful tool for first-generation Ivorian migrants like Remy and Martine. Even though the association's original membership peaked at around 53 people, 25 to 30 people still actively participate. Remy says that his four children, who all live successfully in the Washington, DC area, choose not to be in the association but do enjoy going to the club's parties.

CHAPTER 4
Case studies of clubs with Latin American and Caribbean roots

Struggle and service in Guatemalan *cuchubales*

Transitioning to the United States from Guatemala was an uphill battle for this immigrant. While obtaining documentation, this migrant used a mix of personal savings strategies and cuchubales *to create a financial safety net. This money was used for family obligations and eventually to support a much-needed medical centre back home in Guatemala. This story was written from their perspective by Annie Bright, Kim's former student.*

I was born in Tejutla, San Marcos, in Guatemala. I have five sisters and two brothers, so there are eight of us in total. My youngest brother is also here in the United States. Now, I have two daughters both born here in the US who are 23 and 16. One of them recently graduated from college and the other is in high school. Their education is extremely important to me.

I came to the US in 1997. When you arrive like I did the transition is difficult: much of your life is outside of your control. I didn't have legal documents, so I also didn't own things like a car – much less a driver's licence – and I couldn't work, and I didn't have a bank account. Language, also, was a significant barrier – I spoke almost no English at the time. Fortunately, I found people that took me in like family, many were Guatemalans who had been here longer than me. I continued without legal status for my first 15 years in the US until I learned of a law that could grant me legal status. Nearly $13,000 and two years later, I became a legal resident – and later a US citizen. I didn't have a car to get to my appointments; there were times when I couldn't even eat because all of my money was spent on the legal process. It was worth it, but very difficult.

Now that I have more security I want to help people in the same situation that I was in when I first arrived, and helping people save is a great way to do that. I knew of rotating clubs when I came here, but I was a little bit afraid to participate at first. For me, when dealing with money, integrity and honesty are critical. When someone would tell me I would need to contribute cash to a club, I would think, 'But what happens if someone doesn't pay?' At first, I was invited to participate by someone who wasn't from Guatemala. They weren't family or anything like that, so I declined. But after that, when Guatemalans told me about *cuchubales*, I saw how members were able to save, I decided, 'Okay, let's take a risk'.

Now, I am forming clubs as an organizer. I've formed three clubs so far with 72 members total. Each has a 'number', which determines their place in the weekly payout. Each week, each member contributes $200 and whoever's number it is that week takes the payout. For instance, one group has 20 members with each contributing $200, which means the payout for one member equals $4,000. We go down the list until every member has received the payout – in this example, that would take 20 weeks – and that ends the cycle. We use WhatsApp to send everyone in the club its basic information: the names of members, the order for receiving payouts, the date the cycle starts, and the date the cycle will end.

We will train other organizers as well. We have members not only from Guatemala, but also from Colombia and Brazil. One potential organizer who I am training is like I was in the beginning – a bit hesitant; she joined the club to observe and learn how it operates, and to gain the confidence needed to organize new clubs.

I took personal finance classes when I came to the United States, where I learned how important financial preparedness is. I like to have at least six months of savings in case of emergencies. I've been able to save for emergencies, so now I'm focused on saving more on top of that. Of course, I'll work to have an income, but I'd like to also have the peace of mind that I am prepared for unexpected expenses like illness or if I lost work for some reason, or a pandemic. Emergencies happen. I also don't own a home now, and I'd like to buy a house one day.

When I was studying personal finance, I learned about a different way to save – a more individual *cuchubal*. You start by saving $5 the first week, and if you want to save for a year, you add $5 to the amount saved each successive week, but you lack the commitment that comes with a rotating club. For me, this commitment is critical. On the individual side, I use strategies that make sure I am saving when I get the payout. Mixing my money from the rotating clubs and my salary isn't the best idea for me. To keep things separate, I opened a bank account specifically for my club payouts. I now leave that card at home, and I only dip into that account with intention.

Group members use their payouts depending on their own needs, and it feels good to know we can help with whatever their life situation might be. For instance, one member is very stressed because they are having to pay $200 in interest alone on their credit card. The rotating club helps because her payout covers the interest, and they can focus on paying the principal down with other strategies. It's a bit of relief. It's different for each member. Another member used her club payout to buy a car, while another used his payout to finish building his parents' house in Guatemala. Many members can send money home because of the payouts, including me. The group contributes to my peace of mind knowing that I have money to send home to my parents.

When we form a new rotating club, we tell people who want to participate that there will be a $30 entry fee to help fund different projects. Members have been happy to contribute, and each group funds a different project. Right now, we will use a portion of our entry fees to support the building of a medical clinic near where I was born in Guatemala. Many malnourished children live there, so we want to support them with food and clothing as well. There is a group here in Massachusetts that works with a group in Guatemala to deliver the resources we collect and to exchange photos and videos of the projects as they progress.

I have always liked leadership and service. Apart from my rotating clubs, I have volunteered with youth for many years. And what I like most about my role now leading a rotating club is that, at the end of the day, I know I am helping someone. We are helping group members save, and we are helping these children and their families through the projects we do. We know there is a lot of need in our country, but you need to start somewhere, and we are starting here.

Running a Mexican *tanda* with a partner in New York

Without discipline, a tanda *can leave you feeling burned. This was Lucia's previous experience with a rotating club. However, through the trust she built with her partner Juan, Lucia explains the benefits of a jointly run* tanda. *Here, money is kept safe in a lump sum until it is ready to be used for a specific, planned expense. The author is Anarge Frangos, Kim's former student.*

Lucia was initially suspicious about meeting with me. She was afraid that my questions had something to do with the IRS or the police. Juan, her relentlessly positive tanda co-organizer, convinced her it was safe to talk with me; the fact that their sharing of organizing duties is a highly unusual arrangement is a testament to the partners' trust for each other.

Lucia is the principal organizer and Juan is her co-organizer. Lucia and Juan's co-management is not the only atypical aspect of their *tanda*. *Tanda* organizers are also most often women. The general consensus among women in the White Plains, New York Mexican immigrant community is that 'men are irresponsible. They like to spend money on drinks, on women, or on the street'. Trust and dependability being critical to *tanda* leadership, it is difficult for a man to generate sufficient confidence to act as an organizer under such perceptions.

However, Lucia trusts Juan because her husband and Juan knew each other in Mexico before they both came to the US. Given their long history, she has confidence in him. Juan has the same trust in Lucia. Her husband lent Juan $600 when he was in a tough situation 14 years ago. Lucia explained why this trust is critical. 'It is important that the person who organizes the *tanda* has a good reputation, because it is possible for *tanda* members or organizers to take the money, move to another state, and disappear. Even if the club finds the absconding member, nothing is written down, and there is no way to legally recover the money'.

Lucia spoke from experience. She was once in a *tanda* with many friends, but she didn't know the organizer. This is a particularly precarious circumstance given that the organizer manages the collection and disbursement of club money. 'I had the last number [meaning she was last to receive the payout], and when it was finally my turn, the organizer made up lots of excuses as to why I could not receive it. In the end, she only paid me $400–$500 out of the $2,000 that week's payout'. When Lucia confronted her, the organizer grew brazen, saying, 'Sue me if you want, but there is no proof'. She was right. *Tandas* are based on verbal agreements underpinned by trust and discipline. There is no written contract. Individuals who are defrauded have no effective recourse. For a long time, this negative experience deterred Lucia from participating in *tandas* before joining again with family and close friends.

Lucia and Juan's *tanda* has 18 members; 7 are linked to Lucia and 11 to Juan. Their *tanda* members do not get together as a group, which means Lucia and Juan are the only points of contact for members. Many members don't know each other. Lucia emphasized the level of trust members put in them through a cautionary tale of another *tanda* that operated similarly, with members' only point of contact being the organizer. 'Because members didn't know each other, the organizer was able to tell each member scheduled to receive the payout to wait. Then they disappeared with weeks' worth of club money without ever having distributed payouts to anyone'.

In Lucia and Juan's *tanda*, members contribute $200 a week for a $3,600 payout. Lucia normally takes the first number unless another member needs the payout on that date, in which case she will often swap with them. Lucia and Juan's members are interspersed throughout the beginning, middle, and end. Some members request specific numbers, while others don't have a preference. Members may request one of the first numbers because they need the payout earlier in the cycle, using the payout like a loan that they will pay back through the rest of the cycle. Others request a number towards the end of the cycle because they prefer to contribute for the duration of the cycle and receive a later payout, using it more as a savings method. For added security, new members, who are admitted through a current member's recommendation, are given the last number in the cycle. They must make a full cycle's worth of weekly contributions before receiving their payout.

Members are allowed to trade numbers during a cycle if both agree. Most often, number trading occurs when one member needs money quickly for some unforeseen reason, leading them to request a trade.

The two organizers have different policies for collecting weekly contributions. Lucia sets aside about 12 hours each week to manage the *tanda*. She waits at her house for the members to come and bring their contributions. She gives members the chance to bring contributions on Sunday or Monday to accommodate everyone's schedules. On Tuesdays, she combines the contributions and makes the payout to the designated member. For Juan, some members bring the contributions to his work or house each week. Others give him the money when he comes by their homes to collect it.

I wondered what would happen in their club if a member didn't pay their weekly contribution. Both organizers assured me this had never happened to them as *tanda* organizers, even during the pandemic. Juan acknowledged the risk but said it does not worry him. He knows who his members are, where they live, where they work, and who they associate with, and knows them to be reliable. If someone doesn't pay him, Juan visits them personally to understand what's going on and make payment arrangements. Still, it is understood that Lucia guarantees the contributions of her seven members, who are made up of her long-time girlfriends and her husband, and Juan guarantees the contributions of his 11, made up of his family and close friends from work. This joint liability is why it's so important that organizers only accept members they have confidence in.

Each week, either Lucia collects $2,200 from Juan for his 11 members or Juan collects $1,400 for Lucia's seven members, depending on who is going to receive the payout that week. The *tanda* members use their payouts for many purposes both in the US and in Mexico. In the US, members use the money for large purchases like buying a car, moving homes, or renting a bigger apartment or house. They may also use their payout for culturally significant fiestas like a *quinceañera*. Members also use their *tanda* money to send back to their families in Mexico. In Mexico, they may use the money to support their family, buy a lot, build a house, or invest in a business. Lucia mentioned that it is almost impossible for people in Mexico to save because they simply don't earn enough money.

Lucia explained that she leads *tandas* because it helps her, and the other group members, invest in these life events and purchases. '*Tanda* is a discipline because it is obligatory. Others are expecting you to hold up your end of the bargain,' said Lucia. The *tanda* plays an especially important role for members who are resistant to sharing information with banks, fearing it will be shared with immigration officials. *Tandas* have the potential to keep their money in a safe place until they receive their payout, at which point they can use it for a specific, planned expense, or to accumulate savings.

A *tanda* organizer keeping ties with Mexico

Celia uses strict rules and tight management to govern her tanda *in the US. Always taking the fifth number of the cycle, Celia states that she is a saver and not a borrower. Knowing the temporary nature of their status, Celia's family hopes to spend their money wisely. Celia's case reflects a rotating club with the intention of returning and investing back home in Mexico, rather than in the United States, as other groups have sought to do. This is evident in the disciplined way in which Celia runs the* tanda, *and its focus on saving, rather than planning social events or investing in properties or large-scale businesses in the US.*

When Celia was only five, her father died, leaving her 39-year-old mother to raise their eight children. She didn't return to Mexico until years later when her mother died. This was a devastating loss for Celia. It cost her $8,000 to get back to the US after this trip as at that time she could not cross the border legally.

This tension, of maintaining and deepening ties back home in Mexico while navigating a precarious legal position in the United States, informs how Celia runs and uses her *tanda*.

Juggling jobs at a dry cleaner and restaurant, Celia works seven days per week to achieve her goals. She has purchased a lot in Mexico where she wants to build rental apartments, and she is working towards building her retirement fund. She has family obligations, too: her 22-year-old nephew who wants to join her in the US to work towards building a house for his father and siblings. His mother died of COVID-19, leaving behind him, his father, his 12-year-old brother, and two younger sisters. They don't have a house, so they are living in Celia's house in Mexico. She is uncertain about bringing him. At present, she has heard it would cost $11,000–$13,000 to cross the border, and it is more difficult now than the last time she crossed. She is actively looking for a *coyote* (smuggler) for her nephew so she can calculate the potential cost and route of his journey.

With so much at stake, Celia turns to *tandas* to keep herself from dipping into her savings for more immediate expenses. She jokes that without the *tanda*, in a flash she would spend her savings at the mall. She used to be a member of another *tanda*, but she has been organizing her own *tandas* for the past five years. She says being an organizer isn't too much hard work for her because she is single. People Celia knows form *tandas* either with their family or co-workers they deeply trust, never with people they don't know well.

Her *tanda* has 10 members who contribute $500 each week: three co-workers, four of her siblings, and two others named Leslie and James. She doesn't want more than 10 members because she doesn't want to have more than $5,000 in her house at any time. Plus, the *tandas* she knows with more numbers tend to have a lower weekly contribution; her smaller *tanda* still has a higher payout. Each week, members bring their contributions to her home by Monday night. She keeps the money in a strong box, then delivers the payout by hand to the member whose turn it is that week.

She knows Leslie and James through a mutual friend. By recommending them for the *tanda*, this friend implicitly guarantees their contributions. Celia felt comfortable with them joining. She trusts their mutual friend and she also knows how many days and hours per week they work. Celia explains that people who don't know each other don't want to put their money together, but she has never had a situation where a member defaulted. If a member doesn't have their weekly contribution, Celia will put up the money to complete the payout, but she will wait only two days for their contribution, before fining them. She attributes her *tanda*'s success to her strict rules and tight management.

Celia always takes the fifth number in the *tanda* cycle. Her family always takes the last numbers because they are 'savers, not borrowers'. They prefer to contribute to the rotating club for the entire cycle and only receive their payouts at the end, as opposed to receiving the payout at the beginning of the cycle, in which case the payout operates more like a loan.

Celia doesn't allow members to switch numbers in case of an emergency, though she knows that is permitted in other *tandas*. She thinks this just over-complicates the *tanda* and can cause confusion for her, so the rules don't permit it. 'Rules are rules.' People have to respect the number they chose.

All members participate to save money. As Celia's brother says, 'We are in this country temporarily, so we need to save our money'. Celia supported this sentiment. 'Everyone knows that you should spend for your food and for what you need, and for nothing else. The rest is savings to be put in the bank and not touched.'

At this point in our conversation, Leslie came into the room and shared some of her story. She has been in the US for less than one year. She explains that she is in Celia's *tanda* to save money because she is making payments on a lot she had purchased in Mexico. The *tanda* ensures she gets a payout every two months or so, instead of holding onto smaller amounts that are easier to spend.

The plot Leslie purchased cost $15,000. She makes payments on the land every two months when she receives her *tanda* payout. She contributes $500 a week, and she lives on whatever is left from her earnings from work. She pays $400 per month to live in a three-bedroom apartment with six people and one child in it. A couple and their child share one bedroom, while Leslie shares the other bedroom with another woman. A man named Jesus and his son share the other bedroom.

Leslie is not happy in the US; she misses her son. She wishes he could join her, but it is too risky. He is only six years old. She talks to him every day on WhatsApp. When I said that at least she was making more money during her time here, she responded, 'Money is not everything'.

Tandas and *cajas de ahorros*: Saving and borrowing in Asheville, North Carolina

Maria's tanda *in Asheville, North Carolina is diverse – made up of Mexicans, Salvadoreans, Colombians, and others. Money saved here can be used in a multitude of ways to fit participants' needs. In addition, Maria notes the presence of* cajas de ahorros *in her community, another kind of informal club from which members can borrow while paying interest. The author of this story is Maria Theresa Nagel, Kim's former student.*

Originally from Puebla, Mexico, Maria has lived in the US for 18 years. She has been organizing *tandas,* rotating clubs, for 16 of those years, all located in her same neighbourhood. Maria sees the *tanda* as a way of building a reserve fund or as she calls it, 'a whatever you need it for' fund. *Tandas* can fulfil different purposes for different members. For some, a *tanda* may be the only way to self-finance a car. For others, like Maria, it may be a good exercise in discipline to generate an emergency fund. 'I just bring them their money; I don't ask what they do with it,' she says.

Maria learned from some friends that if she organized a *tanda* herself, she could get the first payout. 'It's like winning the lottery,' she says, 'except instead of risking a loss you're always awarded your savings upfront'. The *tanda* organizer must distribute the numbers to participants, with each number marking a place in the payout cycle. She calls members each week before picking up their contributions. Typically, Saturdays and Sundays are designated as pickup days, and by Monday all contributions have been collected.

Maria's *tanda* will pay out $5,000 each week to one of the 20 members. Some may not be able to afford the $250 contribution each week, so they can partner with someone else and each pay only $125. Each payout is for $5,000. If they make the full $250 per week contribution over three cycles, they will receive $15,000.

Maria ensures everyone contributes on time by only including people she knows well and trusts. If new or less well-known participants want to join the *tanda*, they must be willing to take the last places in the payout cycle.

How does an immigrant afford to save $250 every week? Typically, Maria explains, immigrants in her *tandas* work two jobs. 'We work a lot,' Maria says. Some members work full-time in construction and part-time at a restaurant, while others might sell food or babysit to complement their full-time jobs. In either case, participating in a *tanda* involves sacrificing extra income to save for the future. I asked Maria how she taught people to be disciplined. 'Once they decide to join a *tanda*, automatically people know they cannot spend that money because it is for the *tanda*'. She adds, '*Tandas* keep the money in our community and out of the pockets of rich banking moguls'.

As an organizer, Maria benefits from getting the first number, but she otherwise does not benefit from managing the *tanda*. However, if someone has an emergency and requires a payout, that member will pay Maria to facilitate the new order of payout recipients in the cycle.

Maria's *tanda* work keeps her busy; Mondays are entirely dedicated to driving to members' homes to pick up and drop off their contributions or their payout. As she walked me through a typical Monday, I couldn't help but ask, why go through all this trouble and have the only benefit be getting the first payout? 'I am an active person and I like doing this,' she says, also noting how apparent the impacts of *tandas* has been for her community. 'It's hard for people to understand that we immigrants have an opportunity. It takes saving and seeing the money in their hands to change their mindset. This is what helps them learn.' Maria shared what participants have accomplished with their savings, from buying a trailer to sending their payout money back to Mexico. With the possibility of deportation looming for some, sending money home helps them accumulate savings in case they are sent back.

All members of Maria's *tandas* are Latino – they come from Colombia, El Salvador, Mexico, and other countries. According to Maria, *tandas* are neither compatible nor necessary for those born in the US. 'I think we're educated differently. For them, money works one way and for us, it works another. They have the possibility of going to a bank, taking out a loan, and buying a car. They meet the requirements; we don't.' Most people in Maria's *tanda* have bank accounts, but they don't keep their savings in these accounts. The bank accounts are used mainly to deposit cheques from work and withdraw cash. 'Bank accounts make good business for bankers. *Tandas* make good business for us,' Maria explained.

She says that the area around Asheville is flooded with immigrant-owned businesses, including many taquerias. *Tandas* have funded these businesses of migrants who are largely undocumented. Those who have been granted permission to stay in the US may opt for bank loans instead of *tandas*, but many still use *tandas* to fund entrepreneurial ventures. Maria believes at least 75 per cent of the Mexican population in Asheville participates in *tandas*. 'This is important for me because others can see that they can make their money work for them. They put their money to work and earn something. And that, yes, they can achieve their goals. They can do it.'

In addition to their *tandas*, many in Asheville also participate in *cajas de ahorro*. Like in a *tanda*, members save a certain amount each week. However, instead of contributions being distributed as payouts during the cycle, the money accumulates in a fund. Members can borrow from the fund while paying interest. The interest is split equally among members at the end of the year. Some *cajas* distribute the accumulated savings as well and others allow the fund to keep growing. There are also ceilings on the loan size, dictated by the amount each member has saved. Usually, the limit on what a member borrows is a multiple of their savings, which guarantees the loan.

Maria thinks borrowing from a *caja* is a good idea. She has witnessed many community members suffering from the 10 to 20 per cent interest rates required by money lenders' loans, and the *caja* loans offer much lower rates. Immigrant clubs, like the one Maria belongs to, go unnoticed by the financial services industry, but for the communities involved, they are a pivotal part of their economy and their path out of debt and poverty.

Brazilian *consórcios* offer room to breathe

Penelope, a Brazilian immigrant living in the United States, partici-
pates in a consórcio *group. Everything is coordinated by a trusted*
member, Graça, via phone messages. This system allows members to
save for themselves or send money back home to Brazil. Penelope's
club is a mix of men and women of different professions and incomes.
Common factors include a strong connection either to the coordinator's
family or to a trusted member of the club who has an impeccable
reputation among local Brazilians. No rules require members to
be Brazilian, but all members at the point of the interviews were.
The author is Marcia Mendes, Kim's former student, who is writing
from Penelope's perspective.

I have been in the United States for more than 20 years, but have
only been a documented immigrant for four years. When I came
to this country, things were very different; it was much easier to
get jobs without a social security number. Especially after 9/11,
however, things got progressively harder for undocumented
immigrants. I currently work cleaning houses, apartments, and office
buildings.

I have a bachelor's degree in business management from a
Brazilian university, but I have never been able to work in my field
as my degree is not recognized in the US, and I struggle to learn
English. I can make do with my proficiency, but it would be hard to
get a better job without speaking the language properly. Until my
immigration status changed four years ago, my biggest challenge
was being undocumented.

I have always been a person who keeps a cash reserve. Back in
Brazil, I lived with my parents and I would save at least 25 per cent
of my salary every month in a bank account. When I lived back
home, I had heard of *consórcios*, but only the ones you did through
the bank, never through friends. But here in the US, I learned about
consórcios among friends.

Everything started for me when a friend of mine entered her
sister's *consórcio*. Each share, or contribution, was $200 a week,
which was too high for me, but I decided to split my share into
three: one part was for my first friend, one for a second friend, and
one for me. Then it finally seemed manageable to me, and I joined.
In our split-shares group, each of us contributed $67 every week
and combined it to make the needed contribution. When I got my

payout for the first time, it was wonderful! It got to me just at the perfect time. I got excited about how much I was able to save and decided to stay for the next cycle. However, I always split the share with others.

My motivation to join for the first time was because I was broke and in debt. My car had broken down and I had taken out a loan to buy another used one. At the same time, my husband had been laid off. When I received my first payout, I realized I could pay off my debts and still have money left. I thought, 'This is great!'

For each cycle after that, I had a different objective in mind. For example, one objective was so I could go to Brazil to visit my family. The trip itself was not the issue, but since I would not be working for more than a month, I needed to somehow keep the cash flowing. The year after that, I saved for the down payment on my first brand-new car. My next goal is to save for the down payment on a house.

I have tried to save money by safekeeping it at home many times. However, I could never put together a considerable amount of money, like $3,000 or $5,000. Whenever I needed money, I would go to 'the money pile' and take it out. A broken mirror, school supplies, and Christmas presents were some of the reasons I raided the money pile; I could never reach my objective.

The *consórcio*, on the other hand, is a commitment. That is why I always ask to be last on the list to receive the payout. From the moment I join, I am obliged to put that money away. I cannot just decide that this week I will not set money aside; I must do it. So, that is what I think is most effective. It is discipline. Today, I can breathe more easily because I know with certainty that in a given month, I will receive that sum of money.

I committed to staying in the group after realizing I was finally able to save more money than I ever had before. I don't think I could have saved any other way, even when I could find extra income sources.

Every week our club's organizer, Graça, collects the contributions, combines them, and delivers the payout to a member. I think it is a huge responsibility, and Graça has never charged us for it. There are no profits for her; it is something she wants to do and likes to do because she wants to be in a club with people she can trust. Only people very close to Graça's family or to someone who is already in the group can join. If a friend of mine decides to join the group,

I will need to vouch for them. I have been in the group for five years, and I do not even know what would happen if I vouched for someone and they went AWOL.

This year, our cycle started in November and will go through December next year. Apparently, more people joined at the beginning of this cycle, so it will be a month longer than our typical 12-month cycle. But none of the 40 members in our club has ever defaulted. That's why Graça is very cautious about who can join.

In terms of collection and disbursement, every club I know has a system. Graça assigns a place for us to leave an envelope with our cash contributions. You write your name and the amount of money on the envelope and leave it as per her instructions. Before, she would collect the funds in person, but since she was not always home, she and her husband developed this method of leaving the envelopes in a hidden safe box. On Sundays, the member whose turn it is to receive the payout meets her. She opens the envelopes in front of them, counts the money inside each, and then hands the member the payout.

Positions are assigned through a lottery system and the payout is dispersed every week. Some members have a preferred month to receive the money, and they can ask for specific positions in the rotation, which Graça considers when making the list of payout recipients and dates. It is a straightforward system without many conflicts.

I, for example, choose to be the last in a cycle. I do not like to feel like I'm borrowing. I would rather deposit the money, just like savings, and get the lump sum at the end. So, Graça always places me in the last month of a cycle.

When someone has an emergency and needs to swap their spot because they need the money earlier, they can post on our Messenger group. The person will say, for example, 'Hi everyone, my spot is in April, but I need the money in March. My spot is not so far away, so if someone in March wants to swap with me, let me know'. People will do that out of friendliness. In our group, there are no extra fees. All you need to contribute is your share. People are not even close friends, but no one is looking to gain anything or make any extra money. There is no difference if you get your payout earlier or later; you will get the same amount. I've heard of other clubs where payout amounts vary according to your position in the rotation, but ours is not like that.

Nobody goes to the bank to deposit their $10,000 payout. You keep the money at home. The paychecks you get from work? Yes, those you deposit into your bank account. But *consórcio* money? $1,000 or $2,000 in a bank account would be alright. But to deposit $5,000 or $10,000 – the range of payout amounts – members just do not do that.

We don't meet. We receive a phone message at the beginning of a new cycle. There's a piece of paper with a list of the 40 members. Graça writes down the member's name, their number of shares, and the date when they will get the payout. Then she sends us a picture of that paper sheet. I do not even know everyone in the club. I know only that a few friends of mine are in it. When I receive the list of members for the cycle, sometimes I see some familiar names that I did not know were joining. People I know from the Brazilian community, but also many strangers … I put my complete trust in Graça. She approves people to join the club.

Occasionally, Graça sends us a message through Facebook Messenger about a club that she created. She uses it when she needs to make an announcement, like to say that she will be away for the weekend, so she needs all members to contribute by Friday or something like that. But there is no interaction, no socialization. It is all business.

A lot of people split their share (contribution), and we have a lot of members with more than one share. Some have three shares, but then these are members with a good income. Some people are financially constrained, and they participate in the *consórcio* because it is a way for them to save. And some people want to build homes or buy assets in Brazil, so they join for that. If a member contributes three shares and each is worth $200 then the member is contributing $600 per week. In a month, that's $2,400. People who do that are well-established here in the US.

For me, I can't take the risk of committing to an entire share. There are some cases I've seen where the weekly payment is $250. Ours is $200, and I already think it is too much. It's $800 every month set aside for a *consórcio*. The way I deal with it is like this: there is a house I clean on Friday, and that income is *consórcio* money. I don't even think about it or count on it. I mentally block out that house, so I don't even feel it.

I would honestly recommend a *consórcio* to anyone. If I were to advise someone who wants to start a new club, I would start by telling them to only accept members they trust or the organizer trusts. To create room to 'breathe', start with small amounts of money with a group of trusted people – the benefits are worth it.

Caribbean migrants in Boston and their *susus* and their *sols*

Money clubs are a long-held tradition for the Caribbean community. Within the author's network, women participate in closed, secretive clubs to save. Clubs mentioned in her interviews varied in size from 10 to 60 participants. The author of these stories is Gail Carter, Jeff's former student.

My Barbadian parents knew well of 'meeting-turns' when I posed the question to them. I was amazed to learn this, as neither of them mentioned this term while I was growing up in Barbados many years ago. A 'meeting-turn' or *'sou-sou'* or *'susu'* or *'sol'* or 'partner', as these groups may also be called, is essentially a small rotating club. A group of people get together on an agreed schedule, whether it be weekly or monthly. Since each member contributes the same amount, the length of the rotation will vary depending on the number of members in the club.

During my research and interviews, I observed dedicated and disciplined women who set out to save and help others during the process. The women I interviewed were from Barbados, Haiti, and Jamaica. However, their rotating clubs encompassed women from other countries such as Guyana, Trinidad, Dominica, several African countries, and even the US, although the Americans were initially sceptical of this scheme.

Being new to Boston, connecting with the immigrant community was a bit of a challenge. My friend Sara happily told me, 'Oh yeah, my aunt does that. I will connect you with her'. My hair stylist connected me with her friend, and so on. Interestingly, the children of my interviewees did not participate in rotating clubs despite seeing the commitment and dedication by the older generation. However, some think the tradition will not die out.

Betty moved to the US about 40 years ago and continues to return to Jamaica to help children. She was a disciplined participant in her Dorchester club for 40 years, which included 60 members – mostly Jamaicans – and amassed $6,000 per cycle or more. Though the minimum 'throw', or contribution, was $100, each member could contribute more than the minimum amount.

There were no formal in-person meetings, as in the prior case. Members would simply individually meet the 'banker', the organizer, weekly on Saturdays to 'throw their hand' (as they call making their contributions). The person next in the rotation would collect their 'draw', their payout, on Sundays. For Betty's club, the required minimum 'throw' was $100. But some members wanted to contribute more. For instance, Betty herself contributed $500 a week for the 60-week cycle. Because Betty put in $500 per week instead of $100, she was allowed to get five draws by the end of the cycle. Each member would sign the book when they received their draw. Betty insisted that the crucial criterion for a club's high performance is that 'the banker has to trust you, she needs members who she has confidence in'. The members in turn trust the banker. 'Everybody knows that they can trust me. They know that I don't want anything from them. I only want what God has for me.'

Customarily, the club was closed and secretive. None of the members knew who the other participants were. However, the banker would sometimes invite members to a year-end celebration, allowing participants to discover who they had been saving with over the course of the cycle.

Vivien, a middle-aged nurse, lives on Massachusetts's South Shore, having moved from Haiti about 10 years ago. As the administrator of *susus* of various sizes over the years, she similarly recognizes the trust involved in both managing and participating in such a group. She explained, '*susu* has a high reputation; people understand that you don't play with *susu* money'. This understanding, combined with her long-standing presence as a participant and organizer, had led to her success at managing *susus* and finding participants. 'They call me the mother,' she said. 'I am the person who administers the monthly *susu*'. As a long-time participant and respected *susu* 'mother', members seek to join her club through referrals.

Benefits of being the banker

Betty noted that people give the banker a little cash as compensation for her work. In her club, she receives a one-time tip of about $50 from each member, meaning a $3,000 payment in her club of 60 members. Betty chuckled when asked if being the banker has a financial benefit, acknowledging, 'oh yes, the banker makes money, dear'. Some of the men in the club whom she knows well give her more than $50.

Vivien, on the other hand, told me that very few people give her a tip. She said, 'Sometimes the mother would mention to the group that tips are appreciated', but not always expected. For Vivien, tipping can be culturally contingent; she noted that African participants would sometimes tip her $50.

Advantages of club membership

According to Betty, being a member is a way of saving that is 'better than going to the bank' and getting a loan. 'You are doing the saving yourself, though you are still using other people's money to do so. They use your money, and you use their money. This is a chance-taking thing – it is almost like gambling,' she said with a grin. 'A lot of us benefit from this; it helps us to buy a home. Another good thing about it is that you don't have to pay taxes.'

Betty has a bank checking account, but said, 'The bank puts a paper trail on you. It's hard when you put money in the bank and have to take it out. Borrowed money means there is interest to pay back.' She also appreciates the large payouts the club generates. Joking with me about her earlier years, she explained, 'back when I was in the Caribbean, we did not contribute this much money – one shilling, two shillings'. Thus, she was thrilled to make $5,000 in only five weeks.

The next generation and the future of the clubs

While the first generation of immigrants recognizes the value of such clubs, younger generations – especially those born in the US – seem less keen. Paula, a *susu* member, explained, 'My children think that I am losing money, but I am not', and she continues to encourage youths to participate.

Vivien thinks that once the younger generation gets older, they will have developed confidence in the clubs and their impact, but added, 'I don't trust the younger generation that much. They would have the last hand'. She suggested that members of the young generation start at a small amount of $50.

As a younger person listening to these stories, I realized the benefit of disciplined savings. Why pay interest if you can get a lump sum another way? As Vivien said, 'Yes, there is no growth of your money using this scheme. On the other hand, there is no loss of your money either'.

'Mama Sol' and 'Papa Sol': Trust and savings amongst Haitian immigrants

Haitian sols *are built around trust. Usually, the most trustworthy get the first hand and those least trustworthy get the last. Andre, the respondent, negotiates his position to best address his expenses. This story is by Aaron Steinberg, Kim's former student.*

'I can't believe I'm telling you this,' Andre admitted during our interview about *sols*, a Haitian version of a rotating club. As in all of the other cases explored here, trust and discretion are paramount to the success of *sols*, so it was unusual for Andre to share so much about them.

Andre began using *sols* while living in Haiti and was eager to continue after coming to Boston to join his wife. Unsurprisingly, trust between members and organizers is an essential consideration for those looking to join a *sol*, 'Before you get into a *sol* in Haiti, the first question is: "Who is in it?" If you know that someone has weird behaviour with money, you won't get involved.' Fears over non-payment are considerable given that there is no mechanism to force the violator to pay their contribution.

However, Andre mentions that there are ways to mitigate this risk. 'Inside the Haitian community,' he says, 'everybody will know that a certain person is unreliable'. When a *sol* is being organized, either that person will be excluded or will be given the last payout. This trust requirement incentivizes the formation of clubs among people who know each other. Andre explains, 'People in the same *sol* may know each other in a variety of ways. It may be that we're working in the same place or it may be through an acquaintance in some way. You can make a club among friends. It depends'.

Andre calls the organizer of a *sol* 'Papa Sol' or 'Mama Sol', depending on their gender. He explains how the Papa or Mama Sol takes on greater responsibility but does not reap a greater reward than the average member. 'Being the leader of a group does not mean that you will have the first hand. It just means that you hold the money for everybody, and you're responsible for getting the money from everybody to give to the person who is scheduled to receive the payout.' The first member to receive a hand is often the most reliable for the same reason that an unreliable person would receive the last hand.

Andre chooses to take the last hand unless he has something specific to pay for. 'I have been using my hand to pay for my class semesters. Sometimes I take the first or second hand and I will pay for the semester.' The order that the hands are paid out is not decided as a group in Andre's *sol* – the Papa or Mama Sol decides. However, sometimes the leader will offer certain flexibility in the timing of payment as an incentive for potential members to join. People will often negotiate with their Mama or Papa Sol to get the month that will benefit them most. Andre says that the Papa or Mama Sol may try to incentivize potential members by saying, 'Okay, I am starting a *sol* with 10 members for a 10-month cycle, and I have this month and this month available'. The duration of the *sol* can vary, but members usually contribute every month regardless of the length of the cycle.

If a member needs the money sooner, the leader will call whoever has the hand for the desired month and will negotiate with that member, asking, 'You know what, I have this person who is in the *sol* and they need money in your month, what can you do?' Sometimes they resolve in a creative way, such as taking a half-hand one month and giving the member in need the other half. Then when the member in need gets their payout, they will pay back the half-hand they borrowed. As Andre describes, 'It depends on the flexibility of the member who has the hand at the specific point in time. It is a great way to do things.'

Andre also shared his knowledge about a different type of rotating club that flourishes in Haiti. 'You know, people who sell in the street – they have another type of club that is very vibrant called a *sabotay*.' These clubs are primarily organized by groups of street vendors and are funded by their daily sales. *Sabotays* often include more members and more frequent payouts than *sols,* and the Mama or Papa Sol is usually a store owner. Andre provides an example: 'It will have 30 people, 30 days, and paying 50 [Haitian *gourdes* or US$11] a day, so every day someone is receiving a payout of 1,500 gourdes during the 30-day cycle. The same way that people do it in Haiti, we do it over here.'

While Andre sees *sols* as necessary in Haiti because of a lack of formal financial services, he believes that part of the reason they continue in the US is because of their cultural significance. 'We get that culture from Haiti. Since I started working over here, I was like, "Where is the *sol* at?" Because this is the way to save money.' Even with access to formal financial services in the US, Andre continued using *sols* as much for their sociocultural importance as for their financial benefits.

A striking aspect of Andre's *sol* is that he usually doesn't know anyone in the club: 'They are just numbers for me.' Despite the importance of trust among members, connecting with the Mama or Papa is sufficient for Andre. A contributing factor may be that his current club organizer is his stepmother – his Step-Mama Sol. Given Andre's emphasis on the sociocultural importance of the *sols*, it is notable that there is little social engagement generated by one's participation.

CHAPTER 5

Clubs as a development strategy

So far, this book has focused on what rotating clubs do on their own with no external support. Our cases exemplify how creative, entrepreneurial, and, in some cases, social these clubs can be. Jeff, whose students wrote many of the cases in this book, was curious about what would happen if minimal support were offered to rotating club organizers. Could they be encouraged to train more clubs? This interest took him to two Guatemalan communities in Massachusetts where he had connections from his prior work. He returned from each visit describing steaming plates of Guatemalan food, festive music, and an abundance of laughter. He was inspired by how small inputs and encouragement could produce impressive results. Below, Jeff reflects on rotating clubs flourishing, thanks in part to him, in his own backyard (Kim).

After reading the case studies, you understand that rotating clubs – no matter which name they go by – serve as a hidden financial system. They build both community wealth and well-being. They work because they are based on savings traditions perfected over centuries. Their benefits are clear: they present an almost no-cost, community-managed, widely understood means to mobilize resources and avert high-interest lending as they encourage members to help each other.

Yet, although Guatemalan immigrants know how *cuchubales* work, many haven't joined. Many more would join, we thought, with a little urging, but no one had reached out to them. In this chapter we lay out what proved to be a successful strategy for increasing saving club membership, encouraging rotating club leaders to organize more *cuchubales*. We believe this approach could be used in any immigrant community.

We start with the belief that rotating clubs are viable financial institutions in their own right. They provide a convenient way to amass useful amounts of capital through disciplined saving. Furthermore, we understand that only those who have already organized or participated in rotating clubs have the granular knowledge and the commitment to their communities necessary to organize well-functioning groups.

Within that context, our role as outsiders is to identify local organizations with deep connections in immigrant communities, help them identify local organizers to train new groups, and celebrate their accomplishments. 'They already have the answers, just ask good questions', is our starting point. And it is the organizers, not us, who will lead the expansion within their communities and to others, facilitated with small stipends and opportunities to meet and share knowledge.

By pivoting 180 degrees from our solutions to theirs, our starting point is learning how local leaders are already organizing and managing rotating clubs, thereby strengthening the economic fabric of their communities.

The results are impressive. The nearly 100 members of the five newly organized *cuchubales* in Lynn and New Bedford have mobilized and distributed a jaw-dropping $2.5 m over two years. In 2024 alone, the amount mobilized and distributed in the two cities will reach $1.5 m, nearly $9,400 per member. But when we started it was far from certain that this 'they know how' approach would work at all. What follows is the story of how Sindi, Norma, and Nancy from Lynn, and Estella, Sebastiana, Michaela, and Gloria from New Bedford achieved what they have. They had the support of the Latino Support Network (LSN) in Lynn, the Community Economic Development Center of Southeastern Massachusetts (CEDC), and the non-profit directed by Jeff, Grassroots Finance Action (GFA) (see Relevant organizations at the end of the book for details).[1][2][3]

Where our Cuchubal Initiative began: Lynn, Massachusetts

All great ventures start with a meal. I first met Pedro Arce in the 1990s when I was leading a microbusiness loan programme in New England, called Working Capital. Pedro had worked in banks for decades and encouraged them to deliver their services to low-income communities. In 2022 Pedro invited Jeff to a Palestinian restaurant in Cambridge where he introduced me to Hugo Carvajal, the Director of the LSN. As Hugo, Pedro, and I discussed the Cuchubal Initiative over Turkish coffee and plates of hummus and kabobs,

I asked if Hugo would be willing to use the LSN as a platform to launch the project. He said, yes.

A few weeks later Hugo invited me to a meeting in Lynn at LSN headquarters. I recruited John Hammock, a long-time colleague, to accompany me. In the late 1960s I got to know John when he was the evaluator of the Campesino Leadership Program that I had launched with a group of fellow Peace Corps volunteers in Ecuador. Later, John, when he was Acción's Executive Director, hired me to join the Acción team (see Relevant organizations at the end of the book for details).[4]

The meeting in Lynn was attended by a dozen Guatemalan immigrants; some were *cuchubal* advocates and described enthusiastically how participating in *cuchubales* had helped them pay debts, make a down payment on a house, and advance their businesses. In the words of one advocate, 'I think (being part of a *cuchubal*) makes you feel you are in a community. Someone wants to join a *cuchubal* because they want to buy a car and the bank won't give them money. There are so many procedures to do and many in our community do not have the right papers. *Cuchubales* are a way to support us.' Others were sceptical, 'why should I risk my money if someone doesn't pay?'

The LSN office is based on Union Street, the heart of immigrant Lynn. As John and I walk to the LSN office we pass a barbershop where every chair is occupied by men getting haircuts for a night on the town. The barbershop is flanked by restaurants serving *pupusas*, the famous Salvadorean meat pie, sweet fried plantains, tamales, roast meat, and piles of thick Guatemalan hand-patted tortillas washed down with iced tamarind juice and *horchata*. Across the street is a bakery with an assortment of cakes and pastries where you can buy cups of papaya drenched in chilli. On Union Street English is a foreign language. Fortunately, both John and I speak Spanish.

After the meeting Hugo, John, and I came to an agreement. Grassroots Financial Action and the LSN would each contribute $3,000. The $6,000 was divided between the three organizers, Sindi who was already running a *cuchubal* and was the administrator of a health clinic, Norma, a day care provider, and Nancy who worked in construction. Both Norma and Nancy had participated in *cuchubales* for years.

We gave the three 100 days to start new rotating clubs. We didn't know what to expect; what we proposed has never been tried in our country (or even abroad as far as we know), so wedded are we development professionals to institutional solutions – banks, microfinance, fintech. Informal solutions such as rotating clubs aren't on the radar.

Instead of 100 days it took them just three weeks to do the organizing work. When we returned, we learned that Sindi, Norma, and Nancy had organized three *cuchubales*, one with 30 'numbers' and two with 24. ('Numbers' are different from members because a few members save twice as much per week: $400 rather than $200.) The three used their connections in the community to recruit members. Their link to LSN gave them credibility as each organizer reached out to their personal contacts.

Our 'they will figure it out' strategy worked. Apparently the less we did, the better the outcomes.

Each member of the newly organized *cuchubales* agreed to invest $200 or in some cases $400 per week in their groups as the other *cuchubales* in Lynn did. Even though many lived on yearly family incomes of $30,000 or less, as of our last visit in March 2024 there had not been a single missed payment. In these tight-knit communities not making a payment is 'social suicide'. A missing payment means everyone in the group is shortchanged. Nancy said some even delivered food for Grubhub to make their payments, in addition to the income from their other jobs.

The members make their weekly payments on Friday or Saturday. On Sunday, each member in turn receives a $4,800 payout for the 24 'number' group and a $6,000 payment for the group with 30 'numbers'. A cycle ends when all have received their payouts. In their third cycle, almost all who joined the first cycle are still active and many new members joining. Sindi, Norma, and Nancy are now collecting and distributing $24,000 every week, substantially more than a million dollars a year.

John and I travel to Lynn every few weeks to find out more about how the organizers work with their groups and what they learn working as a team. In their words:

> Norma: It can be seen as a game, because we are playing, but it is delicate, meaning it is a big responsibility. Whoever has an urgent need I give them the first numbers to receive their payout, one, two, or three. There are people who come to me

five months before the end of the cycle and tell me by such a date I need the money to buy a house or a car.

Sindi: We don't put in someone we don't know unless someone else says: 'Oh, he's my cousin, he's known, he's trustworthy', and thank God no one has turned out bad for us .... If they want to leave the group, we look for someone to replace them, but if they leave, they don't lose any money. They are given the money they have saved so far.

Nancy: I have no problem going to people's houses to collect money. What bothers me is when they say they don't have the money. So far, in a day or two they always come up with the money.

The organizers run their groups with flexibility and compassion and a strict sense of discipline.

Showing how seriously they take their responsibilities, during the second cycle Sindi was gravely ill and was in the hospital for weeks. Her husband and daughter made the collections and she made sure they had all the names and contact information in case she was incapacitated. As for the members Sindi told us: 'There was someone who was deported and had to leave town and there were five payments left to finish. He spoke to one of his brothers and told him that he owed this money and the brother continued paying.'

To compensate them for their time the Lynn organizers charge a $50 fee for each number. If, for example, the member has saved $6,000 over the 30-week cycle, they will receive $5,950. Fifty dollars is less than 1 per cent of the total saved. The organizers deposit the fees into a reserve fund in case someone misses a payment (which has never been used). They divide the reserve fund between them at the end of the cycle.

With their payouts most of the members pay down high-interest loans – money lenders, payday loans, and credit cards – and keep as a reserve for future expenses, rent, utilities, and medical bills. The better-off invest in cars, businesses, and housing.

A survey of the members of new *cuchubales* revealed that: 1) three-quarters of the members were women; 2) only 20 per cent had been members of *cuchubales* in the United States, reflecting the scale of the unmet demand; 3) 42 per cent had family incomes of $30,000 or less; 4) four in five planned to continue saving in their groups.

Asked what they liked about their *cuchubales*, most said it 'taught me how to save', with the rest mentioning how they could use the money. In addition, half said they wanted to participate in a WhatsApp group to communicate with other members, learn more about personal finances, and strengthen their links to other members. Half also said they wanted to participate in other LSN activities such as first-time homebuyers' training. From the perspective of the local organizations, organizing rotating clubs provides a way to link to the other services the local organization provides.

Expansion into New Bedford

For some time, I had communicated with Corinn Williams, the Director of the Community Economic Development Center of Southeastern Massachusetts (CEDC). CEDC is based in New Bedford. I knew Corinn when I was directing Working Capital, the microcredit project I referred to earlier. New Bedford was one of the 60 towns in six states where we provided micro-loans through groups organized by local organizations.

New Bedford was a major whaling port from where Herman Melville, who wrote *Moby Dick*, departed on his storied journey. Recently, the city has become home to a large Latino population, many of them Mayans from Guatemala. Most start their lives in America by working in the city's many fish processing plants.

In July 2023 Corinn and I decided to bring the Lynn experience to New Bedford. Her assistant Sebastiana Raymundo called a meeting that was attended mostly by Mayan women, similar to the meeting John and I carried out in Lynn 18 months earlier.

Later, a delegation from New Bedford travelled to Lynn to meet the Lynn organizers to exchange experiences, reflecting our peer-to-peer learning strategy. The New Bedford delegation was so inspired by their conversation with Sindi, Laura, and Nancy that they organized their first rotating club during the three-hour drive back to New Bedford. The 20 members of the new group invest $100 per week in their 'cundina', the local term for *cuchubal*. Each week one of the 20 receives a $2,000 payout. By the end of the 20 week cycle the organizers had collected and distributed $40,000.

The New Bedford organizers recently decided to add a second group, also with 20 members, boosting the amount collected during the second cycle to $80,000. As Corinn, John, and I were talking to a potential donor during a meeting in New Bedford, Sebastiana huddled with Estella, Michaela, and Gloria to develop their strategy for the second group. They decided the organizers would receive the first payouts as an incentive so that they can benefit from their investments early in the cycle. In addition, new members, or those who are not well known, will be the last to receive their payouts. This reduces the risk as they must continue paying until the end of the cycle. Those who pay late are fined $50 with the payment going directly to the person whose payout is incomplete because they didn't pay on time. Unlike Lynn, the New Bedford organizers do not charge a fee.

Over the next five months, the organizers will collect and distribute $80,000 from the two 20-member groups. As in Lynn, John and I had little to do with the strategy that emerged.

The New Bedford members, most of whom had been in the United States for only a few years, are poorer than the group members in Lynn. As in Lynn, only about a quarter of the members had been members of rotating clubs before. Three-quarters had yearly family incomes of $30,000 or less. None had family incomes of over $70,000.

Building on the 'proof of concept' success of the groups in Lynn and New Bedford, CEDC, LSN, and Grassroots Finance Action are planning to deepen outreach in Lynn and Bedford, and expand the initiative to new cities and towns.

Five dimensions of a successful project

In thinking about replicating this model in other communities, these are the five factors that proved to be important in Lynn and New Bedford. First, we work through a local non-profit with deep ties to the immigrant community. LSN offers homebuyers' and English classes and helps immigrants with their immigration issues and getting jobs. CEDC in New Bedford offers similar services and serves as a centre for immigrants in crisis, who need housing and even need diapers. These local organizations are trusted in the community.

Second, we select group organizers who have organized or parti-cipated in *cuchubales* for years, who are trusted, and who have strong networks in the community. Sindi, Norma, Nancy, and the team from New Bedford all fit these criteria. Third, we have simplified the methodology. We ask organizers to do more of what they are already doing, given that the population already understands the nuances of how informal rotating clubs work. Fourth, we let the organizers develop and refine their own strategies. Outside 'experts' are all too likely to impose their own ideas. It's eye-opening but, for most development professionals, hard to let go. It was them, not us, who developed their outreach strategies and modified their approach based on what they learned.

And finally, most importantly, we ask questions, keep learning, and keep listening. We accept the fact that they are in control not us, and that the success of the venture is in their hands, not ours.

The approach used in Lynn and New Bedford provides a simple mechanism to put control over capital in the hands of those who use their savings to improve their lives in ways that they define as useful. Rotating clubs are a low-cost, community-managed way for members to build assets.

The Cuchubal Initiative was built on the belief that immigrants know best how to address their own needs. External funding can boost existing self-help efforts, assisting those who have yet to be reached by existing circles to join new ones as we have outlined above.

Informal savings in immigrant communities

Lynn and New Bedford are local examples of the vast informal financial system that serves as a major source for financing businesses, buying homes, and taking care of day-to-day needs. Estimates of how prevalent informal savings are in immigrant communities are hard to come by, but in some cities access to savings circles is widespread. For instance, a study carried out by the City of New York found that 74 per cent of Mexican immigrants and 69 per cent of Ecuadorian immigrants save through similar informal means. As of 2022 there were approximately 46 million immigrants living in the US. Thus, the amount saved and distributed through this informal financial system could reach scores of billions of dollars every year.[5]

We are often asked, 'couldn't immigrants just set aside the money in a bank savings account or under the mattress and make the payments to themselves?' In theory, yes. But the data is overwhelming that, culturally speaking, rotating clubs are a preferred way to save in many immigrant communities. For example, in the 2013 New York study respondents were adamant that saving clubs were better because it 'forces us to be disciplined, we need to watch every penny to make our payments'. 'It doesn't charge interest.' 'Banking is expensive for the poor in America.' And 'It's my money that I am using.'

Money clubs work because they are based on traditions perfected over centuries in immigrants' home countries. Different immigrant communities, of course, have differences in how they implement their clubs, but three principles are common: The first principle is disciplined savings. The rotating club structure establishes the expectation that setting aside money to make contributions is an obligation, not a choice. The second principle is mutual account-ability. Members can't let the other members down. The third principle is mutual support. Often one member will make a payment on behalf of another, with the expectation that the favour will be returned. Should illness or death affect a member or their household, other members usually are quick to help out. These principles build on the traditions developed by strong communities and close family ties.

The trillion-dollar informal financial system

The rotating clubs that abound throughout the developing world and the *cuchubales* of Lynn and New Bedford are examples of a vast, worldwide informal economic system that mobilizes and distributes a trillion dollars every year, and rotating clubs comprise a $400 bn piece of that. Add to that number the $550 bn in remittances that immigrants send back home. This back-of-the-envelope estimate is based on the field research conducted by graduate students from Brandeis and Columbia Universities with Jeff, combined with data sets we reference under Further reading.

This informal financial system is based on trust among individuals, and it leverages the accumulated money management wisdom of millions of villagers and townsfolk, who lead rotating clubs with similar models in countries around the world.

Encouraged by our experience in Lynn and New Bedford we hope to also expand to spread this model to developing countries. While there are 419 million rotating club members in developing countries, 2 billion people, most of them the poor and poorest, only save a bit 'under the mattress'. Who better to organize them into new rotating clubs than the most community minded and skilled organizers of existing groups? As we did in Lynn and New Bedford, teams of organizers would be recruited and trained through local organizations.

Reflecting on my role in launching the Cuchubal Initiative, I appreciate how different it is from my earlier work. Earlier in my career I designed, managed, and evaluated microfinance projects around the globe as well as in the United States. My teams laboured for months writing manuals, training local staff, securing lines of credit, setting up loan monitoring protocols, logging payments, dealing with payment problems, and evaluating performance. With the Cuchubal Initiative, consistent with our 'they know how' strategy, we have stumbled on this new/old approach to grassroots economic development. We experienced excellent results, at minimum cost, with minimum effort on our part plus a chance to learn from the organizers. The organizers take on the roles of the microfinance team.

Reflections on the Guatemalan experience in Massachusetts

We start by understanding how immigrants are carrying out their own financial inclusion, meaning including themselves in financial systems that work for them. Then we add our skills as development practitioners to facilitate the exchange between organizations and leaders, evaluate impact, mobilize resources, and link to other institutions. In this way, we can build on what the informal sector has already achieved.

If this seems daunting, consider that all disruptive initiatives start small, but as word spreads, they can reach enough scale to have a substantial impact. What is important is starting. We will learn along the way.

Notes

1. Latino Support Network, https://www.latinosupportnetwork.org/
2. Community Economic Development Center, https://cedcnewbedford.org/

3. Grassroots Finance Action, https//www.grassrootsfinance-action.org
4. Acción International is now one of the leading institutions promoting microfinance around the world. Read more at https://www.accion.org/
5. Office of Financial Empowerment (2013) 'Immigrant Financial Services Study', *New York City Department of Consumer Affairs*. Retrieved from https://www.nyc.gov/assets/dca/downloads/pdf/partners/Research-ImmigrantFinancialStudy-FullReport.pdf

Concluding thoughts

John and Jeff recently visited a Guatemalan restaurant in Waltham, a town close to Boston. They asked the waitress if she had ever heard of a *cuchubal*. First, she was amazed that these white guys knew what a *cuchubal* was. Then they asked her if she was part of a *cuchubal*. Once she overcame her surprise she told them that she saved $200 every week. Over the years with her *cuchubal* payouts, she had purchased two houses in Guatemala and paid off debts. Now she was planning to take her son to Spain. Consider that $200 per week translates into $10,000 every year, an amount large enough to finance life-changing investments. The waitress's story could be told millions of times across this country.

This is hardly new. Immigrants – Irish, Italian, Jewish, Chinese – have long taken development into their own hands when they were newly arrived in the United States. They do this through self-organized groups that encourage savings through discipline, accountability, and mutual support, not as rugged individuals pulling themselves up by their bootstraps, countering the Horatio Alger narrative.

Whether we outsiders are aware of it or not, immigrants are moving their lives forward through their own efforts including participating in rotating clubs. Our work in Lynn and New Bedford merely nudged along what was already under way. We hope that the success of this project will encourage others to launch similar efforts.

For us, knowing only the square-box financial world of banks, credit cards, and investment funds, the informal financial system that underpins an immigrant's ability to thrive and achieve the American Dream is a mystery. Yet understanding the informal financial system is not that difficult. It is often just a matter of talking to the driver during your next taxi ride, or, as we did, to the waitress in the next restaurant you eat at about their *cuchubal* or *tanda* or *susu* or *dhikuti*. Once you have that conversation, and many more like it, you will find that all that we wrote about in this book is true.

We selected cases for this book to demonstrate the plentiful variety of clubs in the US. Since they are self-formed, members make the rules and those vary from club to club. The diverse rules reflect the interests of club members. Some set rules that encourage clubs to be engines of business growth. We drew out the example of the Bangladeshi clubs where more than $100,000 a month was coursing through their coffers. Others use them mainly for social purposes. We saw the example of the parties that members looked forward to for the entire year. The Ivorian club comes to mind. Still others hope to diminish the consequences of a financial setback, caused by the death of a family member. The registered taxi *iddir* of Ethiopians in Boston exemplified just how formal an insurance club could become.

Such variety of purpose and structure means there is no right way to form or manage a club, no right way to set ground rules, no right way to pay organizers, no right way to determine the order of rotation (if it is a rotating club), no right way to set loan terms (if it is a savings and loan club), and no right way to determine claims (if it is an insurance club).

But there is a wrong way to do all these things and that's when clubs don't follow their own rules. Members frequently spoke of the 'tough love' that clubs meted out to non-compliant members and believed strict adherence to the rules was necessary for both financial gain and social satisfaction. We saw in the case of the Cambodian clubs that following the rules had become lax and the club suffered for it.

Perhaps the single point that Jeff and Kim would like to drive home is that the sheer energy and force of will applied by immigrants in the US are manifest in these clubs. Clubs are the outcome of financial savvy, diligence, and creativity. They fuel business growth and social cohesion. They produce lasting financial ties, strengthen economic networks, and generate confidence and well-deserved pride. Through them, members are one step closer to achieving the American Dream. In fact, some members declare they are already achieving it. Surely, these clubs are a part of their journey.

Further reading

Bonnett, A.W. (1981) *Institutional Adaptation of West Indian Immigrants to America – An Analysis of Rotating Credit Associations*, University Press of America, Washington, DC.

Demirgüç-Kunt, A., Klapper, L., Singer, D., Ansar, S., and Hess, J. (2018) 'The Global Findex Database 2017: Measuring Financial Inclusion and the Fintech Revolution'. *The World Bank Economic Review* 34 (Suppl._1): S2–S8. https://doi.org/10.1093/wber/lhz013

Gons, N. (2013) 'Immigrant Financial Services Study', New York City Department of Consumer Affairs. https://www1.nyc.gov/assets/dca/downloads/pdf/partners/Research-ImmigrantFinancialStudy-FullReport.pdf

Oh, Joong-Hwan (2007) 'Economic Incentive, Embeddedness, and Social Support: A Study of Korean-owned Nail Salon Workers' Rotating Credit Associations', *International Migration Review* 41(3): 623–655. https://doi.org/10.1111/j.1747-7379.2007.00088.x

Servon, L. (2017) *The Unbanking of America: How the New Middle Class Survives*, Houghton Mifflin Harcourt, Boston MA.

Silva Thompson, L.M. (2016) *Moving from Rags to Riches: Together or Alone? Underground Cooperative Savings: An Ethnography of Workplace Rotating Savings & Credit Associations (ROSCAs)*, PhD dissertation, The New School, Milano.

Vélez-Ibáñez, C.G. (1983) *Bonds of Mutual Trust: The Cultural Systems of Rotating Credit Associations Among Urban Mexicans and Chicanos*, Rutgers University Press, New Brunswick NJ.

Vélez-Ibáñez, C.G. (2010) *An Impossible Living in a Transborder World: Culture, Confianza, and Economy of Mexican-origin Populations*, The University Press of Arizona, Tucson AZ.

Zeller, M. (1999) 'The Role of Microfinance for Income and Consumption Smoothing' [online], FinDev Gateway, Inter-American Development Bank,https://www.findevgateway.org/paper/1999/02/role-microfinance-income-and-consumption-smoothing

Zong, J. and Hallock J. (2018) 'Frequently Requested Statistics on Immigrants and Immigration in the United States' [online], Migration Policy Institute. https://www.migrationpolicy.org/article/frequently-requested-statistics-immigrants-and-immigration-united-states

Relevant organizations

Accion, https://www.accion.org/
Community Economic Development Center, https://cedcnewbed
ford.org/
Grassroots Finance Action, https://www.grassrootsfinanceaction.org/
The Latino Support Network, https://www.latinosupportnetwork.org/

Index

www.ingramcontent.com/pod-product-compliance
Lightning Source LLC
Chambersburg PA
CBHW051258020426
42333CB00026B/3266